20TH CENTURY MAN

By
Carlene Havel

Copyright 2022 by Carlene Havel. All rights reserved.

Cover design by Joan Alley, Mannamedia Services.

Table of Contents

Dedication
Foreword
Chapter 1: Bango
Chapter 2: Saturday with Paw Paw
Chapter 3: 1904
Chapter 4: Papa
Chapter 5: New Mexico
Chapter 6: Moving West
Chapter 7: Bigun
Chapter 8: Cowboy Carl
Chapter 9: Flying High
Chapter 10: Private Carl
Chapter 11: Hawaii
Chapter 12: Surprise, Surprise
Chapter 13: Wedding Bells
Chapter 14: Riding the Rails
Chapter 15: San Angelo
Chapter 16: In Sickness and In Health
Chapter 17: Goodfellow
Chapter 18: This Means War
Chapter 19: Shipping Out
Chapter 20: South Pacific
Chapter 21: Ponam
Chapter 22: Biac
Chapter 23: Peace
Chapter 24: Chief Yeary
Chapter 25: Guam
Chapter 26: Texas Again
Chapter 27: W5YC Over and Out
Billie's Poem
Other Books
About the Author

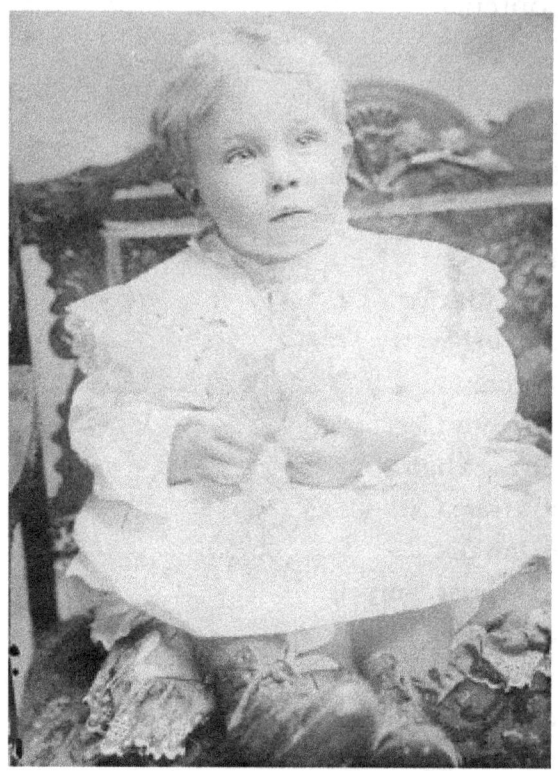

Dedication

For Carl William Yeary and his descendants.

Also, for the millions of ordinary people who survived a pandemic, a great depression, two world wars, and the ever-changing times of the twentieth century.

Foreword

This story came from many sources, including snippets of things Carl wrote during his lifetime and recollections of family members. Paw Paw tape recorded some of his wartime stories, which Bill Yeary (Carl's nephew) generously shared. The facts may not have been exactly the way Paw Paw saw them, nor the way his family remembers his telling of them.

Carl didn't always use good grammar, and he scoffed at the notion of being politically correct. He respected enemy soldiers and, in his later years, developed a great admiration for Japanese electronics and automobiles. He hated no one.

This book uses phonetic spelling of some family names and Pacific islands that could not be located on any map.

Carl flew in PBYs, also known as Catalina Flying Boats, in WWII. They probably weren't as up to date as the one on the cover.

I apologize for any inaccuracies.

Chapter 1: Bango

She thought it was so cute when my first faltering attempt to pronounce "grandmother" came out "Bango". Cute is big in our family, and so the name stuck. Subsequent grandchildren learned it from me. The rest of the clan gradually took it up. Eventually, even her wide circle of friends knew my grandmother as Bango.

The last six or seven years of her life, Saturday afternoon was our time, mine and Bango's. We played cards four hours straight. We were evenly matched, each more keen to best the other than to win a game. We engaged in small talk, mostly comments on strategy or speculation on what was in the others' hand. Family gossip waited for the next shuffle. The unspoken rules required the victor to close the Saturday session by expressing mock disgust at the easy win, solemnly vowing never to play cards again with the loser, who presented no worthy competition. The following week, the game was on as if those words had never been spoken.

We paid no attention to Paw Paw on our precious Saturday afternoons. Bango had been his wife for more than sixty years. I suppose she had earned the right to ignore him when she wanted to. So, Paw Paw listened to the television against the backdrop of our cutthroat card games.

One Christmas, I gave Bango an electric shuffler because her failing hands could no longer mix two decks. Little by little she became less canny at figuring out what cards I had in my hand. Winning lost its pleasure when it came too easily. We gradually regressed to those games whose boxes said they were for children. There were good days when she would cackle at sticking me with the Old Maid and bad days when she was too confused to win although I cheated to her advantage. After we stopped even pretending to play, I did my best to entertain her with silly jokes and sillier talk. She began to include other people in our conversations, people I couldn't see and kinfolks who died before I was born. Towards the end she didn't know who I was any more, nor even who she was.

"Who's he?" Bango asked, gesturing towards Paw Paw.

"That's your husband," I explained. "Carl. You remember him."

She snorted. "That old man's not my husband." She had by then retreated permanently to the comfort of a time when Carl was young and handsome, her children were toddlers, and the people she loved most were still alive.

I don't suppose the hard lessons from the great depression ever faded. Ever-frugal Bango was often heard to say, "Use it up. Wear it out. Make it do, or do without." She never bought plastic bags. Old bread wrappers served the same purpose. At her death, she had an impressive collection of used twister ties, string, paper sacks, and reclaimed mayonnaise jars with lids. She championed recycling before it became a thing.

There is some measure of comfort in the sameness of family funerals over the years. Naturally, Bango's took place in the pie-shaped chapel of the funeral home our family had patronized for generations. It says something about the average age of the population in a town when there are more undertakers than fast food restaurants. Bango and her contemporaries had no fear of death. They dropped by what they called the funeral parlor, often bringing along a few kinfolks. They'd sit down and calmly plan out the details of their own funerals. Paid for in advance, of course. They wouldn't think of leaving their bills for someone else to take care of. It should come as no surprise that the least expensive model was the funeral home's best-selling casket.

For years, I didn't go inside the funereal house of death. Then the steel-spined folks born of pioneer stock in the first decade of the twentieth century began to wear out all at once, and I went there far too often. Tough as whit-leather, that's what my dad called that generation. I'm not exactly sure what 'whit leather' is, but the meaning is clear nonetheless.

Great-aunt Opal's funeral was in the same chapel, a year or so before Bango's. Opal lived her last few years at a nursing home but kept her car parked outside, visible from her window, to demonstrate that she could leave if she ever wanted to. She rarely felt well enough to go to church on Sunday morning. Most Saturday nights, though, she gamely summoned up the strength to go square dancing. Some said her son swapped her casket for a cheaper model and got a partial refund on the funeral package Opal paid for. Others said, no, her son's wife did it. She and Opal never got along. Paw Paw said they were both too dad-gummed bossy, but he voiced that opinion out of Bango's earshot. She didn't hold with criticism of her family.

And Great-Aunt Gladys. Once the nursing home staff neglected to bring her afternoon soda and didn't respond promptly when she buzzed to remind them. She had a perfectly logical reaction. She called 911 to report abuse of an elderly person. The emergency service dispatcher called Gladys' daughter and told her to get over to the nursing home and straighten things out, which she did. Thereafter there were no more calls to 911. No need; the Dr Peppers arrived promptly at ten, two, and four, just as they were supposed to. Attendants from the nursing home came to both Opal's and Gladys's funerals. They hugged the relatives and dabbed at tears during the service. Salt of the earth people populate little Texas towns.

There is a satisfying feeling of continuity that comes with knowing the location of my ancestors' bones. Dobyville, Texas, was settled in the 1850's. The town is long dead, but the cemetery lives on. Civil War veterans sleep there near the graves of people killed in Indian raids, alongside a startling number of Spanish flu victims and unnamed infants.

The historic little cemetery is perched on the side of a hill, on ground where rocks outnumber blades of grass. The few scrawny trees fail to break up the unremitting summer heat. People were buried here a century before it became fashionable to make graveyards look like front lawns. Still, the place never looks run down. Even before the state put up a historic marker, people took good care of the sparse trees and flowers in the old cemetery. My relatives at Dobyville go back to my great-great grandparents, and then my grandmother joined them. If I must bury someone I love, Dobyville is the place to do it.

According to our tradition, Bango's bones rest with her husband's family. She never made any distinction between blood relatives and in-laws anyway. The way she figured it, family is family, encompassing the whole sometimes sorry lot, superseding all other priorities. She can be at peace in Dobyville. She will again know who she is. And if spirits engage in such lighthearted frivolity, she will clean their clocks at Gin Rummy.

Chapter 2: Saturday with Paw Paw

My Saturday afternoon talks with Paw Paw had an exact starting point. I am not entirely sure why I went there the first weekend after Bango left us. I did not want Paw Paw to think I came to their place only to see my grandmother, even though that was the truth. As much as anything, after years of a set routine, I didn't know where else to go on Saturday afternoon. So, at the normal showing-up time, I found myself at Paw Paw's door. More sophisticated people might call his dwelling a mobile home, but he and Bango always referred to it as a trailer. It was a bargain, always of paramount importance to survivors of extreme poverty. My dad spent several times what they saved on the purchase price to fix up the trailer and try to make it tornado-proof. After a lifetime of restlessness, Paw Paw settled into a place anchored into the ground with big steel cables.

Daddy poured a little concrete pad for Paw Paw's radio tower. Out in the county, at least in those days, people built a barn or added a room to their house when they felt like it. Building permits were for city people. When the concrete dried, Paw Paw did the rest of the setup for his ham radio operation. He ran the wires, connected his transmitter, and checked all the calibrations. Everything was in perfect working order when he finished, an outcome he never doubted. That's not bad work for an eighty-five-year-old blind man.

Paw Paw was legally blind for twenty-five years by the time he and Bango moved to the trailer. He had an ever-diminishing sliver of vision left, what he would describe in military fashion as the space between ten and eleven o'clock. He said if he sat at exactly the right distance and cocked his head just so, he could make out most of the TV screen. When I came in that first Saturday of his time as a widower, he switched off the television. Mild discomfort overtook me when I realized that must mean we were going to talk.

In our family, we generally do not have long discussions. Men note that rain is, or is not, needed. Women exchange recipes and home remedies. The more important something is, the less likely it is ever to be mentioned. Therefore, I wondered what in the world Paw Paw and I would find to talk about all afternoon. I mentally addressed the question of how soon I could leave without being unkind. I was in for many surprises, about to discover what scant information I had about this man I thought I had known all my life. I can be such a fool.

In my earliest memory of him, Paw Paw was dressed in a Navy uniform, and we were walking down a street in Los Angeles, California. The year must have been sometime in the 1940s. Even though the sidewalk was three or four times as wide as any I had ever seen, it was crowded with people. And they were in a hurry. The casual, strolling gait we practiced in the small Texas town where I lived was enough to get a small child trampled on the streets of L.A.

"What are you doing?" the grownups kept asking me. I did not know how to explain that if I bent over the toes of Paw Paw's shoes, I could see my face in them. I had certainly never seen my reflection in the steel-toed work boots my dad wore. I sometimes snuck into my mother's closet and played with her purple suede platform high-heels, but even those marvels of modern fashion didn't act like a mirror.

Paw Paw stayed in the Navy as long as he could. During their years of world travel, Bango longed for home. When he retired, out of consideration for her, they settled down in a little Texas town not far from where they started out. It was the kind of place big city Texans, say from Dallas or Houston, wrinkle up their noses and call a "one-horse town." However, Bango was rock certain everyone would live in her home town if given a choice.

Exotic locales had loosened Paw Paw's ties to his birthplace, but he managed to settle into the local routine. They shopped around, bought a duplex, and lived in both sides. One of the living rooms became the guest bedroom. That made three bedrooms and two bathrooms, all at a bargain price. The extra kitchen evolved into a storage area where things sat in a haphazard array of cardboard boxes and old grocery sacks. The functioning kitchen sported a well-worn yellow plastic and chrome dinette set, upon which yummy cobblers, hot homemade bread, and wildly competitive games of Canasta were regularly served up. The unfinished attic contained Paw Paw's electronic gear. He would retreat up there for hours, oblivious to heat and cold. His powerful ham radio took him around the world to talk to anyone on the airwaves interested in swapping a few sea stories. Carl Yeary was, and always would be, a voyager.

A door between the two bathrooms doubled as a passageway between the duplex units. It was crucial to remember to lock both doors if you wanted privacy in either bathroom. Good manners also dictated remembering to unlock both doors upon departure. Anyone on the wrong side of a locked bathroom was supposed to exit the house, go around, and re-enter what was called 'the other side'. Generally, though, they beat on the bathroom door until someone heard the ruckus and let them pass through into the other half of the house. Knowing whether the bathroom was truly occupied or the last person out had simply forgotten to unlatch the second door was a delicate matter. Grandchildren were known to take the closed bathroom door as a sign they should start pounding on it—often to the chagrin of one of their half-deaf great-aunts ensconced on the toilet. Proper house etiquette was to announce plans to take a bath well in advance to everyone, particularly in bad weather, to avoid trapping someone on the wrong side of the house.

Bango worked as a volunteer at the Senior Citizen's Center until she was seventy-nine, cooking and serving food to folks she called "them old people". Between meals, she regularly trounced all comers at dominoes. As time passed, her and Paw Paw's fierce commitment to independence was no longer enough to sustain them. There were plenty of relatives in the little town they lived in. But that's not how it works, at least not in our family. When you get old, cousins, nieces, and siblings do not take care of you because that's up to your kids.

Paw Paw and Bango reluctantly considered the eighth decade of life to signify oldness, and agreed it was time to move closer to one of their two grown children. After due deliberation, they opted to go further south to be near their daughter, my mother. Their duplex was sold to a man who planned to house his family in one side and a sewing machine repair business in the other.

I don't know if we have more rules than other families or not. I just know we have them. They are not written down, and are hinted at rather than clearly stated. Absorbed, more than taught. Everyone gets married. Everyone who can has children. Men work hard and support their families. Then they die first. Always. A few of the rules slowly changed over the course of the years. The kids now buy things on credit, for example. There have even been divorces among the grandchildren. The clear assumption was that Bango would face her final years of life as a widow. Paw Paw never expected to do without her.

As Saturday afternoons went by, I learned to my surprise that Paw Paw kept up with everything from the Loch Ness Monster to the operation of the

International Monetary Fund. He never hesitated to tell me for whom I should vote in an upcoming election, and why. One Saturday he talked in precise detail about the pros and cons of financial trusts. My favorite times were when he would tell me adventures from his life that started almost a hundred years earlier in a town that died before he did.

Wait. I'm starting to ramble on like one of my great uncles. If you really want to know Paw Paw's story, we should start at the beginning and let him speak for himself.

Chapter 3: 1904

I am the son of William Yeary and Lela May Cook Yeary. Some say our family name was once O'Yeary or O'erie, or even Youree. I believe it's Irish, because Mama used to say we were as Irish as Paddy's pig. But one of our relatives did some research and said our ancestors came to this country from Scotland. Somebody else said that didn't matter, that the Yearys were Irish, but lived in Scotland. So, I don't really know for certain.

The first Yeary I know of for sure was a John Yeary, born in eastern Virginia in 1796. From there, some of the family moved on to Tennessee, with a few of the descendants finally ending up in Texas in the 1820's. I know my grandmother on Papa's side was real proud to be one of the Warners of Virginia. Supposedly, her family thought grandpa Calaway Yeary wasn't someone she should marry. So, they eloped, with her riding double with grandpa on his mule to get away.

My mama and papa married in 1898. I was born in November of 1904, out yonder in Naruna, Texas. My folks had just recently returned from the Indian Territory where they had been for a year or so. I was born in Naruna shortly after they returned. There's nothing there anymore. Over time the town dried up and blew away like a Texas tumbleweed. I had two older brothers and two younger brothers. Mama had five boys before my baby sister Bessie finally came along. Curtis was the oldest of us kids. Mama said Curtis was fine at first.

We moved to Lake Victor, Texas, around 1905, when I was about two years old. They had built a railroad from Burnet to Lampasas and started the little town of Lake Victor. There wasn't really any lake there. I was told the town name came from trains making a stop there to take on water.

My father moved his medical practice to Lake Victor and we lived there until about 1909 or 1910 when we had a place built up around where Ira Hutto lives, or I guess now Ira Hutto's daughter. The old place was still there last I knew. I used to go by and see it now and then just to see if it still looks natural. We lived there for a few years and about 1914 we moved to a place east of Lake Victor. It was the old Boyce place, on the headwaters of the Gabriel River. It was just a creek where we were, but a little further down it became a river that runs down by Georgetown. We lived there in Lake Victor, and I started to school there when I was seven years old. The old school house is still standing. It was later remodeled and made into a church. The Lake Victor community building is what was originally the old Methodist Church.

My folks were living in what we called a shotgun house when Curtis was born. That's a house with a hall right straight down the middle, running from the front door to the back door. You'd generally have one or two rooms on either side of that main hallway. Mama told me when he was about a year old, Curtis was sitting in the hallway of that shotgun house one morning when a whirlwind came through. She said the wind swept him out the back door. He landed on his head and was never quite right after that. That happened way before I was born, so all I know is what Mama told me. Papa never talked about why Curtis was different.

Calaway, grandpa's namesake, came along about three years later, then me. So, it was Curtis, Calaway, and Carl. I guess they ran out of C's, because the next child that came along was a boy they named Ralph. He was a little more than three years younger than me. Ralph and I were always close. After Ralph, Don and then Bessie were born. Until I was a teenager, I never knew anything but good times. I reckon I took everything for granted.

I was always closer to Papa than to Mama. Everybody I knew called their parents Papa and Mama because that was the fashion back then. I would have laughed at any boy that called his father "Daddy".

By the time I was born, Papa had a pretty good medical practice built up. After he finished school, he studied for a while with old Doc Howell in Burnet, Texas. I guess you'd call that being an intern.

Papa had an office in town there in Lake Victor, but not that many people came to his office. He made rounds in his horse-drawn buggy just like doctors today make rounds in a hospital. There were folks who were chronically ill, and he called on them regularly. If a person took sick suddenly, the family would send for Papa and he would go where they were right then.

There was a druggist in Lake Victor, too, what you might call a pharmacist today. Papa sent some business to the drug store, but mostly he bought ingredients from there. He liked to mix a lot of his medicines himself, in his office.

I remember one time some of us were swimming in the stock tank near the road on our property when we spied Papa's buggy coming up the road. I can't tell you why we thought this was a good thing to do, but someone suggested we moon Papa. Now if you don't know what "mooning" is, it's basically showing your bare hind end. We didn't have any swimming trunks to get out of, since we always swam naked. So, we were all crouched together on the side of the bank that faced the road. We took turns peeking over the edge of the bank to time things right, laughing like a bunch of hyenas.

Pretty soon, Papa's buggy was passing right by the bank of the water hole. So, at the critical moment, we all raised up together, our backs to the road, bent over with our hands holding on to our ankles. What we didn't know was that Papa had a nurse riding in the buggy with him. She had come to help him do some surgery.

Later that evening Papa gave me and Ralph a good talking-to about mooning when we didn't know for sure who was going to see us. But I could see he wasn't really mad. In fact, he seemed to think the whole thing was a pretty good joke on us. Ralph and I turned red and tried to hide our faces anytime that nurse came in the room. Papa said her only comment on our little show was something to the effect that it must be pretty rough country around Lake Victor. A woman had to be right hearty to make a nurse of herself back then, and I guess this old gal was no exception. Mama never brought up this incident, so I don't think Papa or the nurse ever told her. She would have been mortified.

Papa bought one of the first automobiles around that country, but it never gave him any good service. It might have been a good car in the city, but it was never made to withstand the rough roads we had around Lake Victor. Finally, he junked it and bought a Model A. Now, that Model A Roadster was one dandy car.

Chapter 4: Papa

After the great flu got started around Lake Victor, Papa caught it. Mama kept trying to make him go to bed and stay there, but Papa wouldn't hear of it. He said there were too many sick people that needed his help. Papa was the only doctor for miles around.

The night before he died, Papa got up in the middle of the night to go and deliver a baby. Somebody came by the house and said there was a Mexican woman trying to give birth but she was having trouble. So, he went. He was already sick before he left, but he was real bad sick when he got home early the next morning. Mama sent for the doctor from Burnet. Old Doc Howell came, but it was too late. There probably wasn't anything he could have done anyway.

I remember Papa laying in the bed coughing up blood. He raised up, looked around and saw Ralph and me crouched down by the foot of the bed. He said, "Somebody get my boys out of the room. I don't want them to see me die." Right after he said that, some relatives made Ralph and me go in the other room. That was the last time I saw Papa alive. It must have been early December, 1918. He was forty years old.

I think Papa was a good doctor for that day and time. He went to medical school in Fort Worth. Then he served an internship under Doc Howell over at Burnet. He wanted Papa to take over his practice there, because Doc Howell wanted to quit doctoring and go into the banking business. Papa tried living over there in Burnet, but he just couldn't stand being that far away from his people. That sounds foolish now, I guess. It's probably only 15 or 20 miles from Lake Victor to Burnet. But that was a whole day's trip by wagon back then. So, after a year or two, Mama and Papa moved back to Lake Victor.

Papa had his own instruments and mixed a lot of his own medicines. Doctors did that back then. I remember him telling Grandpa Yeary, his father, that he needed to exercise some. After he quit running cattle on the ranch, Grandpa just sat in his rocking chair by the fireplace and looked out the window. Papa told him if he kept just sitting there, pretty soon he wouldn't be able to get out of that chair. He was right. Grandpa got so he couldn't walk before he died.

Papa was real proud of the fact that he never lost a mother in childbirth. A couple of times he lost the baby, but never the mother. He told me once that people with pneumonia sort of drowned. Sometimes he would go in there through their side, puncture a lung and draw out some of that fluid. He tried it on some sheep first. When it worked and the sheep survived, he decided to try it with people who were so bad they were going to die if he didn't do something. He saved some people's lives with that technique he thought of.

One time I remember a fellow coming to the house to see Papa. The man had sugar diabetes. I guess you call it something else now. Papa told him what to eat and that it would be a good idea to walk a lot. After the man left, I asked what was going to happen to him. "He's going to die," Papa said. That was before anybody knew anything about insulin.

Papa always made a good living, a real good living. Sometimes people would come around to the house for him to treat them, but most of the time he went to where they were. When I was younger, he had two fine horses named Grey John and Polly. I think they knew they were good-looking animals, from the way they sort of pranced along instead of just walking Lots of times, he'd want me to ride with him if I wasn't in school. It was always good to go places with Papa. I guess our family was what you might call "prominent" today.

When a doctor went to call on a patient back in them days, he was expected to stay a while. I'd say Papa's shortest stay at a house would be two to three hours. Of course, if it was close to mealtime we would be expected to stay and eat with the folks. It would have been considered an insult if we had turned down the hospitality of a meal. I always enjoyed eating at somebody else's house. Some of them had lots of good food, and some of them didn't have much to offer. But whatever it was, they were always ready to share it with us. Papa never let me hang around right where he was actually treating anybody. Kids had to stay out of the way. If a baby was being born, the men folk had to pretty much skedaddle, too. Lots of families would have some old man—about like I am now—living with them. Most of these old boys were either ex-Indian fighters or Civil War Veterans. A lot of them wore long hair, and usually had long, flowing beards. I spent many good hours sitting around some farmhouse table, listening to those old codgers tell stories about the things they'd seen and done.

I remember one old man whose hands stuck out from his body at an angle. He told me he broke both his wrists when jumped off a cliff to get away from some Indians. I never did know why they were after him, or even if the story was true. He sure knew how to spin a yarn, though.

Papa let me go with him anytime he could. People in Lake Victor showed my Papa a lot of respect. I loved riding in his buggy, nobody but me and my Papa riding along in that fancy black buggy with a top on it. The top looked kind of like the tops of baby buggies looked before everybody got to using those stroller deals.

Papa would talk to me just like I was a grown man when I went with him in his buggy. There were no radios to listen to, and no signs alongside the road to read. I remember him telling me more than once, "Son, when you go out to face the world, you'd better put on your fighting pants. If you don't, you'll end up with mud on your Sunday britches." I served a purpose on those trips, too. I opened and closed the gates. Most everybody who lived on a spread of land out in the country had a gate on their road. The gates were more to keep the livestock in than to keep people out. Country people loved to have visitors back then. Travelers brought news, and people were hungry to know what was going on in the outside world.

I remember one night coming home with Papa when he was very upset. He'd gone to deliver a baby, and I knew it had died. Papa told me he had to crush the baby's head to save the mother. Otherwise, he said, it was never going to be born and the baby and the mother were both going to die. He couldn't quit going over and over it on the way home. I didn't know what to say, but I could tell he hated the whole business. He never mentioned that incident again after that night, and neither did I. I still don't know if he ever told Mama or not.

Kids that grow up with two parents don't know how lucky they are. I was fourteen when Papa died in 1918. After that everything changed. Papa had a little book where he recorded what people owed him, but Mama never asked any of them for any kind of payment. She said they'd pay up if they could. A few good folks made it a point to see that we got what they owed. Sorry to say, most seemed to think Papa's dying meant their bill was paid in full. Then some real low-down scoundrels beat Mama out of everything we had. Mama didn't have any business sense at all. I was the oldest son at home, except for Curtis. Even though he was grown up physically, Curtis could never be any help. Calaway was married and had his own wife and baby to try to feed. So, it fell to me to take care of the family. I tried hard to keep going to school, but before long I had to quit.

I never did know for sure why Mama left Lake Victor. I remember some men from the family told her she had to put Curtis in the insane asylum. He wasn't crazy, but he was hard to handle. Mama cried over Curtis for a long time before she gave in and had him committed. At first, Mama talked about bringing Curtis home to live with us some day. I thought it might happen, but later on I realized we were never going to be able to take care of him. When we were packing up to leave town for good, I heard Mama tell one of her friends she was sick and tired of men folk telling her what to do all the time. Maybe Curtis was the final straw. Or maybe she made up her mind to be poor in front of people she didn't know instead of folks who remembered when she was the town doctor's rich wife. Anyway, she never said why, and I never asked.

Now, my little brother Ralph loved to farm. It was the only thing he ever wanted to do, and I guess he was pretty good at it because he did it all his life. My childhood was cut short but Ralph never had one at all. Years later, when he got kind of prosperous, some banker from Lubbock told Ralph he ought to let the bank manage his money for him. Old Ralph just laughed. He said, "I made it by myself. I think I can manage it by myself." That banker should have known he'd never get in Ralph's pockets. He had been through too much to be careless with money. Mama and hard times taught all of us how to take care of whatever we had.

***

Almost eighty years after his father's death, I found a small wooden box in Paw Paw's cabinet. It appeared to be an old cigar box. Inside were an old-fashioned shaving brush, a straight razor, and a stack of birth certificates signed by Dr. J.W. Yeary. "What is this?" I asked.

When I described the box, Paw Paw slowly reached out both hands for it. His fingertips moved lightly over the box's contents, stopping to caress the bristles of the shaving brush. "These were Papa's things."

Paw Paw had carried those precious keepsakes across oceans, through decades, over a lifetime. In the old man's face was the fresh, aching loss of a fourteen-year-old boy. I never before heard such tenderness in his voice. "My Papa", he whispered. Again, he softly repeated, "My Papa."

Chapter 5: New Mexico

I had my fourteenth birthday in November of 1918. That was right before Papa died, and I found out since then there was some connection between the flu epidemic and the big war. Nobody called it World War I back then because everyone was sure there would never be another fight that involved so many countries at once. The old civil war veterans around town said civilized nations would never take the risk of another big war. They said modern weapons like poison gas were so horrible that another worldwide conflict would wipe out the whole human race.

Other than worrying some about some cousins who were fighting, Mama didn't talk much about the war. She was never interested in politics. I don't think most women were in those days, not the women I knew anyway. When I was little, it seemed to me Mama spent most of her time planning parties. After Papa died, she was too busy trying to hold our family together to think much about what was going on in Europe. I remember the local boys sported some mighty fine-looking uniforms when they came home.

I needed a job right away after Papa died. I started working pretty regular at the cotton gin right about then. It was hard work. The man that ran the gin said if I was going to do a man's work, he would pay me a man's wages. He didn't actually pay me as much as the grown men that worked there, but he did give me more than I made working as a farm hand. I hated everything about farming, and I was ready to do anything that got me out of the fields. My brother Ralph said there was something satisfying about putting seeds in the ground, watching a plant sprout, and nursing it along to produce ears of corn or a mess of beans. I never saw much percentage in it myself. To me, farming is just something that has to be done so people can eat. I know of nothing else to recommend it. Anyway, while I was working to get us some cash, Ralph was doing what he could to grow crops on our land. Calaway was away at college and of course Curtis wasn't allowed to get out of the house unless one of us went with him. I don't think Curtis was retarded, but he didn't have any sense, no judgment at all. Mama and the two little kids picked some cotton while I was working at the gin. It hurt me to see their hands all sliced up and bleeding from fighting cotton bolls all day, but I never said anything about it.

Work was harder to come by in the wintertime. I didn't know exactly how tight things were for Mama, but I knew she was watching every penny. Old Boss Warner came by one day and asked Mama if I would be interested in going to New Mexico with his son Jim, to stake out a tract of land as a homestead. It wasn't as glamorous as going to France, but at least it was a chance to see more of the world than Lake Victor and get paid for doing it.

Mama wasn't too keen on the idea of New Mexico. She thought Jim Warner had been kind of wild before he went in the Army and she didn't like the idea of me being in his company without her able to see what was going on. I didn't say anything when she fussed about Jim. I figured from the start we couldn't afford to let the opportunity pass, and it turned out I was right. As soon as the wildflowers started sprouting, Jim and I set out in a covered wagon loaded with supplies. Now, travel back then was a lot different than traveling is nowadays. We didn't have hotels, highways, and restaurants everywhere. You carried your food and expected to stretch it out by hunting for game along the way. You had a water barrel that you filled up when you started and replenished when you could from clean streams or maybe some farmer's well. Anything else you needed between home and where you were going, you carried in the wagon.

There were no superhighways with signs every few miles telling you where you are or how far it is to the next gas station. In fact, what few gas stations existed were in towns. There wasn't much need for them, back before everybody and his brother had a car or two. Back then you had to know the way to where you were going, or if you had money you might hire a guide. Poor folks traveled on a trail. In our case, we picked up the old Santa Fe Trail and followed it all the way to the mouth of the Rio Puerco River. What we called a trail was a set of deep wagon ruts that went across open country. At the end of the trail, you'd find a town with a rail head where cattlemen shipped beef on the hoof to market.

I guess it took Jim and me two or three months to get to the Warner homestead in New Mexico. We took turns driving the team and walking alongside the covered wagon. On a good day we probably covered twenty-five miles or so. The oxen were steady enough, but you couldn't hurry them like you can a horse. The trail sometimes wound around a little, too. It would take us around hills and ravines and through the best places to cross canyons and rivers.

Jim and I entertained ourselves by talking to each other. There was a lot more good conversation back when people didn't rush around so much. We didn't have radios or anything like that. So, we enjoyed the scenery along the trail and Jim told me all about the things he'd seen and done when he was in the Army. I was mighty impressed that he had been all the way across the ocean and back.

When daylight started to fade, we would make camp. We'd find a good spot to stake the animals where they could graze. Then we'd build a little fire and rustle up something to eat. Mostly we ate beans and hardtack, which is something like a dried-out biscuit. Jim would spin yarns about his time overseas. To hear him tell it, he split his time between almost getting killed and courting French ladies.

Jim had a rifle he brought back from the war. He showed me how to disassemble and clean it up real good. Of course, I already knew how to shoot better than Jim so he didn't have to teach me anything about that. All farm boys went hunting with guns back then.

We slept under the stars, in our clothes. People nowadays think they have it easy, living in air-conditioned houses. But they don't know how good it is to have the sunrise wake you up on a cool morning, no sound anywhere except the birds singing and maybe some breeze rustling the grass. Nothing is better than a deep breath of clean, good-smelling air. I would get up, wash my face and comb my hair. Mama would never allow her kids to come to the breakfast table without clean faces and combed hair. By the time I was fourteen, it was a well-established habit to clean up as soon as I woke up. That's not to say I would take a bath every day if I had to wash in a cold stream with lye soap. But I always washed my face and brushed my teeth first thing of a morning. Still do.

Jim would make coffee and hitch up the oxen while I went and tried to get us something to go with our beans that night. I got us quite a few rabbits and squirrels, and sometimes a bird. I bet you never tasted a squirrel. I've always thought it is the best meat there is. One morning all I could find was a possum. Now, possum meat is no good at all. It's tough and greasy, but I shot one and Jim and I ate it.

Jim never got tired of talking about the Army, and I never got tired of listening. He explained how you could recognize a man's rank by the stripes or insignia on his uniform. He told me all about military things like general orders and special orders. He would call cadence while I marched next to the covered wagon. By the time we got to Cuba, New Mexico, Jim said I could follow drill orders as good as any soldier he ever saw.

I stayed a week or so helping Jim get things set up on his homestead. I had taken my horse up there with me, and I worked odd jobs for some of the other homesteaders. Then I sold my horse, took my saddle and caught a ride back to Albuquerque about 125 miles away, where the railroad was. Bought me a ticket and came back home. I came back and worked in the cotton gin there in Lake Victor that fall.

I was kind of sorry for this trip to end. It was the biggest adventure I'd ever had up to then, seeing a lot of Texas and New Mexico for the first time. But I needed to get home so Mama could collect my wages from Jim's father, Boss Warner. He was our distant kin, but he still had to know I had finished my job before he paid up. That's how old Boss Warner did business. He didn't get rich by trusting people to do right.

Chapter 6: Moving West

At first, we tried to farm the place there in Lake Victor. Then Mama got a notion to move out on the Plains. She sold that place in Lake Victor for a lot less than it was worth and we moved west, out near Morton, Texas. We came real close to starving out there on the plains.

We made the move around my seventeenth birthday. I guess that would make Ralph fourteen, Don eleven and Bessie seven or eight. We loaded all the stuff we were taking into a railroad box car, which we almost filled up. We took a team and wagon along with about two hundred cedar posts, which came in handy when we arrived there. I rode through with the baggage in what people called the immigrant car back then. Mama, Ralph, Don and Bessie went on the passenger train to Littlefield where we unloaded our stuff and stored it in a wagon yard.

Since I had just recently completed a trip of about a thousand miles in a covered wagon from Lake Victor to Northwest New Mexico, I thought I was the one to be wagon boss of the trip to the new place near Minnie Veal on the Old Slaughter Ranch. We left Littlefield and went by the Old Yellow House Ranch headquarters, where the tall windmill was. The problem was, I had never been to where we were going and Mama had no idea which way to go. Fortunately, we came in by the Old Prairie Dog Windmill near where Rufe Bennett lived. He gave us directions. We camped out one night somewhere between the Yellow House Ranch and Rufe Bennett's place. Now this was the middle of November, and it could have been very cold, but the weather stayed nice. Like the old saying goes, God takes care of fools and children. We arrived at the place which was just raw land. There we were, a widow woman with a bunch of kids and no barn, no house, no shelter of any kind.

A couple of days later some of the new neighbors came over and dug a half dugout and I think Rufe Bennett took his Model T Ford Truck and went to Littlefield and hauled out the lumber to put a top on the half dugout.

Do you know what a half dugout is? It's something like the Indians used to live in. First, you dig a hole in the ground the size you want your dwelling to be. Then you put a little short wall that looks like a bunch of fence posts around the edge of the hole you dug, leaving an opening so you can go in and out. Attach a roof to the posts, and there you are.

In a half dugout, you use the earth as the floor and most of the walls. You build up some dirt from the floor to make a ramp that reaches up to the gap in the posts where you go in and out. With a quilt or flap of cowhide over that entryway, you're in business. I think our half dugout was probably fifteen feet square. That might sound small, but it seemed huge when we were digging it out. It was plenty of space for the five of us. Mama cooked on a wood stove that sat in one corner.

A half-dugout is dark, but it keeps you warmer in the winter and cooler in the summer than a house that's all above the ground. That means you don't need as much wood for heat. Wood is scarce out around Morton, Texas. So, it was a good thing we brought those cedar posts with us.

When I look back at our move, I know that it was not the best planned affair and I guess the Good Lord just took care of us. I do remember there was some bad feelings between the cattle ranchers and the new settlers which the cattlemen called nesters. And I can understand that now because the farmers were threatening the cattlemen's way of life and building a new one for the farmers. Our relatives back in Lake Victor were dead set against us going to Morton, but Mama could be stubborn as a Georgia mule once she made up her mind on anything. She was a little bitty woman, never weighed more than ninety pounds in her life. But her will was strong as any man's, once she set it on a purpose.

I remember our first Christmas in that half-dugout. We didn't have any crops yet because we just got there a month earlier. We were barely scraping by on what I could bring in doing odd jobs. For a while, I didn't have steady work, just picked up a day or two here and there. I couldn't stand it that Christmas was going to be just another day for the kids. Ralph and I were old enough to understand, but I could see Don and little Bessie were never going to have the kind of Christmases we had when Papa was alive.

I was lucky enough to catch a ride with a neighbor going into town on Christmas Eve. I spent the two pennies I had in my pocket and got two peppermint sticks. Back then a one cent stick of candy was big enough to last all day if you just licked on it. You know, if you didn't get greedy and start taking bites out of it. It probably seems strange now to think how proud Ralph and

Mama and I were that we had something for the little kids the next morning. It made Mama cry to see how excited Don and Bessie were. At least they knew it was Christmas.

Like I said, I hated farming. I'd do anything I could to keep from doing it. That's how I got to be a cowboy. I'd work on the ranches around us for wages and leave the farming to Ralph. Together, we managed to keep going and put food on the table for the little kids and Mama.

Chapter 7: Bigun

My best friend in school from the first grade on was Bigun Shelby. When he was born, they didn't think he was going to make it. So, they didn't bother giving him a name. His Daddy looked him over and said "Well, he's a big 'un, ain't he?" After they decided he might live, they gave him a proper name. But it was too late by then. Nobody ever called him anything but Bigun, even in school.

We went to school in the building that's now a country church house. It's across the street from the community center where we used to have family reunions in Lake Victor. There was a big partition that would fold down to divide the auditorium into two rooms. Us kids would roam around all over town at recess and the grownups would complain that we were a nuisance.

We were told never to play in the field across from the school, but we all went over there anyway. One day Bigun and I got this idea to have some fun. We got out there and strung a wire between two trees, right where a bunch of the girls would always run back into the school yard from that field. Then we sat over by the school house and waited and giggled.

Sure enough, when recess was over, the girls came charging through there and fell down in a big pile. None of them were really hurt, but most of them cried anyway. I don't think anybody ever found out who did it. We'd have got walloped if they had. I have an idea we would have thought it was worth it. At that age, Bigun and I thought it was pretty good business to torment girls. Well, Bigun went on and never did have any luck with women. He married three wives, and separated from every one of them.

Bigun's grandfather was a Civil War Veteran. Old "Cap", short for captain I guess. He walked like a duck, with his feet turned way out. His job during the War was to supply the Army with horses. He used to laugh and say it was just a license to steal. He owned lots of good land around Lake Victor after the War.

Mama used to let us collect hen eggs and sell them or trade them. I remember one Saturday Bigun and I got some eggs and headed for town. We were probably about eight or nine years old. For some reason I was carrying the eggs in an old paint can. I remember it didn't have a handle, so I was just holding onto it by the sides. Bigun and I went to the bakery and traded eggs for cookies. They made these real big cookies there, and man they were good.

Well, we came out of the bakery eating our hot cookies, and there stood the town bully. He was a pretty big kid, four or five years older than us. He grabbed a cookie out of my hand and crammed it into his mouth. He looked at Bigun's cookie, and I guess he didn't want it because he slapped it out of Bigun's hand into the dirt. I would have let him have my cookie without saying anything. But when he slapped Bigun's cookie away, it got me real mad. Before I gave it any thought, I swung that paint can as hard as I could. The jagged edge caught that kid right above his ear and split his head open good. I figured he was going to kill me then, but he just ran off bleeding and crying.

But that wasn't the end of it. Pretty soon, here came the sheriff walking up. He asked me if I had split this kid's head open, and I said, "Yes sir, I did." Real solemn-like, he told me to come with him. We walked along for a while, with him not saying a thing. I figured I was going to jail, and I was plenty scared.

When we got a little ways away from the bakery and around a corner, the sheriff said, "You better go on home, now. I guess it was about time somebody taught that kid a lesson." I imagine somebody told Papa what I did, but he never mentioned it to me. Nowadays, parents would probably get sued over something like that.

There were a lot of years when I couldn't get back to Lake Victor. But when I did get to go there, I always went by to see old Bigun. When he got on in years, he told me that when he was young, he did whatever he wanted to. Then after he got old, he just did what he had to do. He lived right around Lake Victor all his life. He's always been a good friend. Reliable, you know what I mean? The kind of guy who would go to bat for you anytime, no questions asked. He just had hard luck when it came to women.

***

A few people who were not at my grandmother's funeral show up at the Dobyville graveside service. One of them is a white-haired, tottery old man, leaning heavily on his walking cane. He plants the cane with meticulous care and slides one foot forward. With obvious effort, he slides the other foot even with the first, and advances the cane another few inches. As he makes dogged progress, I think someone has taken leave of their senses to let this elderly gentleman outside on such a hot, humid day. It takes an exceptionally long time for the old man to settle himself into the folding metal chair next to Paw Paw.

"Carl," the old fellow rasps.

"Bigun." Paw Paw smiles for what seems like the first time in weeks. "Thanks for coming."

By then they had been buddies for almost a century, and Bigun was still demonstrating his loyalty. Thank you indeed, Mr. Shelby.

Chapter 8: Cowboy Carl

I was always pretty good with horses, and that finally helped me get a fairly steady job as a jingler at a ranch near Morton. A jingler takes care of the horses for the other cowboys. Jingling was how you usually started out learning to be a cowboy, or wrangler. In those days, people didn't come to work in the morning and go home every day after work. You wouldn't even get there before you had to turn around and come back again. I lived with the other ranch hands in a bunkhouse. Not only did I get paid, I had meals provided instead of eating food Mama and the kids needed. On the trail, we slept right out under the stars.

The nearest town was what became Morton, Texas, named after Morton J. Smith. I never cared much for the plains. I worked some for Slaughters, and some up at the LX ranch near Amarillo. I worked for old Lee Bivens up there. And while I was working for Slaughters, we went over into New Mexico. They had some land over there around what was known as the six year outfit. We went over there and was branding and so forth in the fall of the year and they gathered 65 head of cattle to take over to Roswell New Mexico. They had some salt grass farms along the Pecos over there. What they would do, they would fatten these cows up and sell them to the butchers over there. All the cowboys wanted to go, of course. I figured there wasn't any point in thinking about it because I was sure they weren't going to let me go. So, we cut out that sixty-five head of stock. Everybody knew old man Louis Probst was going to go and take the herd, but we didn't know who he was going to take with him. Ed Greene hollered and said, "Hey, Kid, come here." I came over there and he said, "You're going to Roswell with Louis Probst."

Man, I was walking tall then. We didn't have a wagon or anything. Of course, we had a pack horse we packed our gear on. We went on over by the Ainsworth Ranch, what's now the crossroads, but there wasn't anything there then. After we left the homestead area, there was hardly any fences. If we came to a fence, we just took it down, drove the cattle through, and put the fence back up again. That was customary then. It took us several days to make this trip. You couldn't drive very far because you had to stop and let the cattle graze. It was the fall of the year and the stock had all been taken off the ranches down there. The cattlemen had mostly gone broke. So the grass was lush and green.

Them old cows would graze all day and at night they'd just lay down. We'd watch until they went to sleep, and then we'd just go to bed. We didn't have to stand night herd on them. The next morning we'd find some of the cows had gone grazing around. And, of course, there you could see them for a long way. Anyway, the next morning we'd get them back together and move on.

Now, there was only one place where we could water the cattle between where we went off the cap rock there and the Pecos River. It was a good little jump across there. And there wasn't all that much to eat around there, either. Anyway, we got them to the Pecos River, and had a little trouble crossing them there. Those cattle had never seen a bridge, and we couldn't get them on it. So, we had to let them ford the river instead. Old Man Probst was afraid there was some quicksand in there. As a matter of fact, there was. He told me, "Don't you let your horse get in there and get bogged down in the quicksand." He said, "Don't worry too much about the cows. We'll try to get them across."

While we were trying to get across, one of the cows broke up the river. I took out after it, riding an old horse called Skewball, a bay. This cow came to an arroyo and she turned down towards the river. Old Skewball, he went across the arroyo, and made a few jumps and came back across the river. He almost lost me there. Anyway, we ran this cow down and chased her over a bluff about ten feet high. and into the river. I thought Skewball was going to jump over after her. I could see the river over his head. But he finally stopped. This old cow hit the water—believe it or not there was water in the Pecos River back then—and the old cow, the stupid critter, wouldn't go on over to the other side of the river. She came right back to the side where we were. I had to go get her and make her cross the river.

Old Man Probst was really mad. I was afraid to get too close to him. I was afraid he would take his catch rope and try to strike me with it or something. Anyway, we got these cows across the river and delivered them to these salt grass farms. We stayed a day or two to let the horses rest up, and then we came back.

On the trail, if another cowboy came along hungry, you'd always feed him. Some of them might have been outlaws, but we didn't ask questions. Beans, mostly. We ate lots of beans. I recently heard somebody on one of those radio talk shows, asking if you could make biscuits without an oven. I called in and told them, "Yes, sir, I've had many a sourdough biscuit cooked in an iron pot over a campfire." They were good biscuits, too. Food cooked over a wood fire has a taste you can't get any other way.

I remember one time up north of here, we were driving our cattle alongside another herd. Off and on that whole drive, we had been having trouble with those other cowboys. One night, some strangers come along and ate supper with us. Real quiet bunch of fellows. Next morning at breakfast, the trail boss was saying he figured men from the other rancher's herd stole about twelve head of cattle off us that night. We talked about going and taking them back, but the trail boss said no, it wasn't worth maybe getting somebody killed over. Well, one of the strangers said they'd go help us get our cattle. The trail boss wasn't too hot on the idea, but he finally said okay. I didn't go with them, but the way I heard the story was, when they got there the herd was on the move. These guys rode out in front of the cattle, fanned out, and just waited there. You know, when they aren't stampeding cattle won't go past a bunch of mounted men. So, the herd stopped moving forward and just milled around. Some of the cowboys came up from behind the herd to find out what the problem was. They rode up and faced the mounted strangers, who just stood their ground.

One of the cowboys said, "You boys looking for trouble?"

One of the strangers said, real quiet-like, "We want them 12 head of cattle you stole."

Then the cowboy got kind of nasty and said, "And just who do you think you are coming around here making accusations?"

Well, sir, the boss of that gang said his name and at the same time flipped his duster back to show his cocked rifle.

The man next to him raised up his rifle and said, "We're mighty pleased to meet you."

The way I heard it, they never finished introducing themselves. The cowboys got real polite and told them to just pick out any 12 head of cattle they wanted. There wasn't a shot fired. I guess it pays to have a reputation.

The strangers didn't stay around. They just gave us back our cattle, thanked us for our hospitality and moved on. Later, Mr. Probst told us those men were bank robbers, but they seemed like pretty good old boys to me. They didn't have to put themselves out for us, but they did.

You know how you see in movies the cowboys ride into town like a bunch of yahoos and raise a ruckus? Well, a lot of that really happened. The first thing most cowboys wanted when they got into town was a bath. Every town would have a bunch of bath houses. You could tell a man who'd just recently got off the trail. He'd smell good, have a fresh shave, and have on new clothes. When you got a bath, you'd just throw away the clothes you wore on the drive.

I knew an Irish woman who built up a pretty good business going around collecting the clothes the cowboys threw away. She had a big, open iron kettle in her back yard. She would build a fire under that kettle and boil the cowboys' castoffs to get the trail sweat out of them. Then she would sell the clothes to poor people who couldn't afford anything else.

I did a lot of growing up while I was working as a ranch hand. Living in the bunk house with a bunch of cowboys, I learned a lot too. They knew about life, how to get along in any circumstance, when to stand and fight, and when to swallow your pride. Some of them were ladies' men, and some of them had no use for women folks whatsoever. But as long as a man was honest and did his share of the work, the other cowboys would respect him.

Those men weren't educated, but that doesn't mean they weren't smart. Now and then one of them would make a fool of himself, though. We all do that from time to time. I remember one ranch owner. I guess he was in his fifties, what I considered at the time to be an old codger. Well, his wife died, and he started courting some young woman barely in her twenties. Real pretty girl. You'd think that old man would take one look in the mirror and realize that little gal wouldn't have given him the time of day if he hadn't had some land and a few hundred head of cattle.

But, no, that rancher thought that girl was just as crazy for him as he was for her. Pretty soon, they turned up married. All of us cowboys gave her a wide berth when she moved into the ranch house. She had flirty eyes, and we knew it would cost us our job if the old man saw us joshing with her. Well, wouldn't you know it? She tried to kill the old man. Poisoned him within three months of them getting married. He lived through the poison, just barely. Right away, the girl packed up and left the ranch. I don't know if that was her decision or his. Anyway, we never saw her again. The boss man didn't seem to hold a grudge against her. After he got well from the poison, he said an old fool like him should have known better from the start. I don't know if he ever got married again or not. It seemed to me he could have found some widow lady his own age that would have improved his life on the ranch. But it could be that poisoning incident soured him on women.

I worked some at the Yellow House Ranch, up around Palo Duro Canyon. A lot of things you see out of Hollywood may not be authentic, but most of the cowboy and Indian movies have at least some basis in fact. The end of Palo Duro is a natural box canyon, but not like you see in cowboy movies. It had an entrance on one side of the box, and the other three sides are high bluffs. You might think if you drive a herd in there, it's just as good as having them inside a fence, but that canyon is miles and miles long. There are lots of caves and unusual rock formations in there.

Saturday was pay day on the ranch. The foreman or some trusted agent would show up with a cash box. The cowboys would line up and one-by-one and get paid in cash. We wouldn't have known what to do with a paper check. Everybody dealt in cash or trade goods back then.

I loved cowboy life, but it has its drawbacks. The work is hard, but that never bothered me. I was used to working hard. In those days, a man expected to work hard. It was just the way life was. The pay was fair, but the problem was the work wasn't steady. You never knew when something would happen and you'd be out of a job. A rancher might get too far into debt and have to sell off his herd. That meant the cowhands had to move on. Most times you'd get paid, but if a man went bankrupt you might not. Weather might get bad. A winter ice storm or summer drought would thin out the cattle, and that meant the rancher had to thin out his work force. It wasn't any more chancy than farming, maybe less so. There was always a lot of risk in both farming and ranching.

The other big disadvantage to being a cowboy was that you pretty much had to give up on family life. You lived in the bunk house or on the trail. The only time you went home was when you were out of work, and that didn't make for a joyful homecoming. I started listening to the cowboys talking about other ways to make a living. I found out I could make as much money as a soldier as I could cow punching. Plus, the Army pay was guaranteed. Once you got in, you served your hitch without getting laid off. The way the boys talked in the bunk house, Army life was tough, but no worse than being a cowboy. I remembered how much Jim Warner loved the Army, and he was in the service during wartime. The war was over and we all thought there would never be another one like it. But the thing that swung me over was the idea that the

Army would send me somewhere I hadn't been before. I always had that longing to travel and see the world. The more I thought about it, the more the Army sounded like a good idea.

Chapter 9: Flying High

Boys coming home from World War I would go from town to town, charging people for airplane rides. Well, one day, one of them came to Lake Victor. You could see him circling down, closer and closer. Everybody ran outside to see what was happening. When the plane landed out in an open field, everyone in town just crowded around, trying to get a good look at it. I don't suppose any of us had ever seen an airplane up close before. I sure hadn't.

This good-looking young pilot said he would take anybody who wanted to go up for a ride for ten dollars apiece. Ten dollars was a lot of money back then, but I didn't have to think it over. That was before Papa died, so I had ten dollars to spare. I ran and got my money and went for my first airplane ride. I wasn't one bit scared.

People seem to either love flying or hate it, and I always loved it. Always. It was so peaceful, up there in the sky, looking down at everything. Even in wartime, I loved getting up there in those PBYs. It's a feeling you can't really describe too well. Man, I'd love to get up there with two good eyes just one more time and have a look around.

Now and then you hear somebody talk about being alone. I'll tell you what alone means. It's flying over the Pacific Ocean at night, just one plane over all that water, no land or lights or even another airplane in sight. That's how it feels to be completely alone.

Paw Paw told true stories for the most part. Occasionally, after some outrageous narrative, he would laugh, slap his knee, and say, "You know, of course, that was a sea story." His idea of a sea story, I came to realize, is the equivalent of what most Texans call a 'tall tale'. It is a made-up story that starts out sounding plausible but ends with a twist no reasonable person would believe. A sea story, like a tall tale, is never told for the purpose of deceiving. Rather, it is a form of entertainment.

Pilots generally love to fly, but most of them seem to hate just sitting round. During the war, they'd have alerts when the pilots had to go out and sit in their planes. Sometimes they'd wait for hours for the all-clear signal. So, some of the smart fly boys trained monkeys to sit up there in the cockpit wearing a helmet. If somebody came by, it would look like there was somebody up there. Wouldn't you know it? One time while they were pulling alert duty, they got the signal to go. I'm here to tell you them monkeys flew the best mission the squadron ever had.

Now that reminds me of a story of the three bulls. There was one big, old bull, a normal size one, and a kind of smallish little bull, and all three of them were walking down the road. The big bull spied a pasture with a bunch of cows in it. So, he decided to stop off and pay the ladies a visit. The other two bulls went on for a while. The normal-sized bull saw a big pile of hay. So, he decided to stop and have something to eat. Now the little bull, he just kept on doing down the road, all the way to town. That just goes to prove a little bull goes a long way.

Chapter 10: Private Carl

I worked for Lee Cooper off and on there in Morton. Then in July of 1924, I joined the Army. More than anything else, I wanted to see the world.

First, I tried to join the Navy. I went and took the exams and everything. But Mama wouldn't sign my papers. I had already told them how old I was. So, they wouldn't let me in. Then I got smart. I went to the Army recruiting office and jacked my age up to 21. They didn't ask for a birth certificate, which a lot of people didn't have back then anyway. Or maybe they weren't as particular as the Navy was. It seemed to me like they would have enlisted just about anybody that came along.

The Army put me and three or four other recruits on the train that same night and sent us to Fort Bliss, near El Paso, Texas. I guess they'd been recruiting all up and down the line. At Fort Bliss, there was an old sergeant there who was meeting all the troops that came in on the train. Well, he seemed old to me back then. So, he started yelling, telling all the recruits to assemble in one area. I heard the recruiting stations had notified him by telephone or telegram how many people were coming in and everything. He got us all together and attempted to march us down to an area where they were going to put us all up in barracks for the night. They cut my hair and gave me a couple of shots, and fooled around. I didn't get any uniforms at that point.

The next morning, they had a bunch of soldiers assembled there who'd been through basic training and were ready to ship out. Someone came and got me and gave me a paper sack. I asked what it was and they said, "That's your chow to eat between here and Fort McDowell. You're going to California."

So, I fell in with a group of guys. They marched us down to the train and loaded us on. I don't know how long it took, but it seemed like a long trip to San Francisco. I did my best not to sleep while I was on that train. I didn't want to miss a minute of that scenery going by. When I got there, I inquired how to get out to Fort McDowell. Some other guys were headed there, so I got in with them. We went on over to Fort McDowell on Angel Island, where they had an East Garrison and a West Garrison because it was a shipping out point as well as a recruit assembly point. The recruits went to the East Garrison.

Young men were buzzing around like a bunch of bees on a hive. It seemed to me I had never seen so many young men my age in one place before, and I probably hadn't. There were sergeants directing traffic, hollering at everybody to go here and do this or that, or get in some line and stay there. They issued us uniforms and a rifle and everything. Well, I knew how to put these uniforms on. I knew how to take a rifle down because Jim Warner taught me all about the Army on our trip to New Mexico. He'd got out his gun and taught me the manual of arms and all that.

Anyway, when I got to Fort McDowell and got my issue, I went back to the barracks and put on my uniform. Of course, they had a lot of things to do like give us some more shots. One thing and then another. I learned right off to call the place where we slept a barracks, not a bunk house. But to tell you the truth the barracks wasn't all that different from being with the cowboys on a ranch. It was a little cleaner, with running water in the bathrooms they called latrines. One difference was that I was no longer a kid being looked after by the older men. Even though we were all kids in the barracks, we thought we were grownups. I guess each one of us was a little uneasy but trying to act like we knew the ropes.

I got right to work cleaning the grease out of my rifle. I don't know what I thought I was going to do with it, but I cleaned it up anyway. I took it all apart, laid the parts out on my bunk, and fixed it up like new. When I got my rifle like I wanted it, I took out a uniform and put it on. I knew how everything went together because Jim Warner had taught me. I went outside and marched around, by myself, in my fresh new uniform with my cleaned-up gun. The folks there probably thought I was nuts, but I was happy to have those good clothes and that nice weapon.

Some of the men bellyached about having to get up so early the next morning. I figured they must be city boys. Farmers and ranchers got up before daybreak where I came from. Country doctors did, too. They had chores to do before they got going on their daily business. The Army fed us what I thought was a real nice breakfast although some of the men griped about that, too. Regardless of what the other fellows said, I decided I liked military life pretty good so far.

As soon as we had breakfast, somebody yelled at us to get our gear together and get ready to move. The soldiers passing through from one assignment dressed in their uniforms, of course. I did, too. I liked my new clothes and I was proud that I knew how to wear them. The rest of the new men on their way to basic training all put their civilian clothes on that morning. As we went pouring out of the barracks, there was a sergeant telling everybody where to go. He was sending the recruits to get on a bus to go to basic training. I started to follow the man in front of me when the sergeant bawled out, "Where do you think you're going?"

It took me a minute to realize he was talking to me. Though, for a fact, he wasn't exactly talking. It was more like screaming. I stammered around trying to figure out what to say. The sergeant glared at me and said, "You get your sorry butt on that bus to the ship." Only he didn't say butt.

I had no idea what bus or what ship he was talking about. I started trying to explain that I was a brand-new recruit and was supposed to be going to basic training. He didn't listen to more than a couple of words before he started yelling again. "You do like I told you, soldier!" I got myself in the line with the other uniformed men as fast as I could, hoping I wasn't about to get in trouble. It slowly dawned on me the sergeant thought I was a seasoned soldier because I was wearing my uniform. Those other new recruits hadn't had Jim Warner's schooling like I had.

There was a bunch of us there on Angel Island. They marched us down to the dock and loaded us on what they called a water boat. It was a boat used to haul water because they didn't have any fresh water on Angel Island. I never could figure out why they put an army post out there. All those men and everything and no fresh water except what they hauled in. I guess later they put pipes out there, but at that time they hauled water in a boat, or a barge-like affair, and pumped it out to the water supply there.

We went over to the docks at San Francisco and they loaded us on the U.S. AT Cambria. AT stood for Army Transport. The Army had two transports in the Pacific at that time, the Grant and the Cambria. And the Navy also had two, the Sherman and the Henderson. You might find sailors on the Army transport, and sometimes—not many—but a few Marines. And there would be sailors going on the Navy transports as well. I was a little bit nervous. More than anything, I was over the moon excited because one of the fellows told me the ship was on its way to China.

Well, these Army transports were manned by civilians, but they had some military personnel, what they called the troop command that took care of all the troops. We all went below and stowed our gear. The next day some time we came up to watch them sail out the Golden Gate. There wasn't any Golden Gate bridge back then. In fact, there weren't any bridges there at all. It was all ferries across the bay. It's hard to believe it now. You see all those bridges around the bay, but they haven't always been there.

There weren't any computers back then. Everything was done with typed rosters of who belonged where. So, it was the next day before they realized they had an extra man who wasn't on anybody's list. By that time, we were well out to sea. Somebody came and got me and said the First Sergeant wanted to see me. He was one crusty-looking, tough-talking old codger. He couldn't have been more than forty years old, but he looked old to me then. His name was Richardson. He'd been in the Army for a long time. Later on, I found out he spent some time at the International Settlement in Shanghai. He'd been in China and the Philippines and all over the Far East.

"How did you get on this ship?" He threw in a couple of extra words, too, the kind you might hear around a bunch of cowboys.

I said, "What do you mean? I just marched on here, like everybody else." Him and his assistant sat there and listened with their arms folded wearing poker faces as stern as any trail boss I ever came up against.

He said, "Well, you haven't been to basic training yet. And furthermore, you don't have a destination." I already knew that, but it didn't seem like the time to say so.

They sat me down and talked about me for a while. The First Sergeant said he would decide what to do with me when we got to Hawaii. Meanwhile, they assigned me to the troop command as a messenger.

That was back before you had electronic communication devices on board ships. So, I spent my time running from one officer or noncommissioned officer to another one, relaying whatever I had been told the message was, and waiting for a reply. It wasn't difficult duty. I worked hard to do whatever I was told and didn't waste time moving between the people I was sent to see. When we got to Hawaii, I was certain I would be put ashore and sent home, maybe discharged or even court martialed if they decided this whole mix-up was somehow my fault.

Nobody said anything about me leaving when we put in to Hawaii, and I didn't ask any questions. I kept on delivering messages around the ship. I was burning up to ask the First Sergeant what the deal was. On the other hand, if my status had slipped his mind, I didn't want to be the one to remind him to get rid of me. I didn't get to see anything of Hawaii. After a few days, I could tell from the messages I was delivering that we were getting ready to put out to sea again. I was real happy when I felt the motors rev up and the ship started putting distance between herself and the shore.

The ship went on out to Hawaii, Guam, the Philippines, Hong Kong, and Shanghai and then came back. I didn't see much of China, but I can always say I've been there. I got off the ship and put my feet on the soil at least. We were there just long enough to pick up a bunch of men who called themselves "China soldiers." They had been guarding the Trans-Siberian railway up in Siberia since the occupation of Germany after World War I. I thought I had seen rough before, but those China soldiers beat them all. They talked rough and lived rough. I guess they had earned it, though. China was about as mean an assignment as an American serviceman could draw at that time. They were a pretty wild, rugged bunch.

I got to be pretty good friends with the clerk in the office. He asked me what I thought they were going to do with me when we got back to San Francisco. I said, "Man, I don't know."

He said, "Well, you haven't had any basic training. So, they're going to have to send you somewhere for that. Everybody has to go through basic."

I said, "Yeah. I guess that's what'll happen."

Then he asked me, "How would you like to get off at Pearl Harbor, in Hawaii?"

I said, "Man, I'd love it. Do you think we can do that?"

He said, "Well, we'll see what we can work out."

I just left it at that. I figured the less I said about it the better it would be.

Right before we got back to Hawaii the second time, headed back to the States, the First Shirt sent for me. First Shirt is military slang for the First Sergeant, just like the captain of a ship is called "The Old Man". You only use these terms when you're around other soldiers or sailors. You would never call the First Sergeant a "First Shirt" to his face, not unless you wanted to get yourself in some hot water. Anyway, I figured this was just another message delivery assignment. But no, the old sarge looked up and asked me, "Yeary, how would you like to stay in Hawaii?"

I didn't hesitate one bit before answering that I would like that just fine. He cracked a smile and said, "Get your gear together and I'll get the orders cut to assign you to Fort Shafter." He kind of looked down at some papers on his desk. "We'll forget all about that other thing. I never had a case like this before, but we'll make a soldier out of you yet." It was all I could do not to jump up and down and holler.

All told, I ended up spending almost thirty years in the military. I never did go to basic training.

Chapter 11: Hawaii

So, in Hawaii they just threw me right in with the rest of the group. Shoot, I could march as good as any of the rest of them. I knew nearly as much about Army life by that time as them guys did, maybe more than a lot of them.

Everything was laid back and casual in the islands back then. Nobody was ever in a hurry. Folks took things easy, and that included the Army. We were on tropical routine, meaning we just worked half a day. In the afternoon you could go swimming or go to town or do whatever you wanted to do. The Army gave me uniforms to wear, a place to sleep, and all the food I wanted. Besides that, they had recreation rooms and theaters and all kinds of other facilities all around there. You could play baseball, whatever you pleased.

My job was guarding prisoners. I got to the stockade about six in the morning and pulled guard duty until noon. All I had to do was keep prisoners from escaping. None of them ever tried as far as I know the whole time I was there. Of course, it could have been real bad if one of those guys had gotten away. The rule was, if you were guarding a prisoner and he escaped, you served out his term. That kept us on our toes, especially the time or two when we had a man sitting there under a death sentence. I don't know if the Army would have actually executed a guard if a murderer got away from him, but I sure didn't want to be the one to test it.

Can you imagine? Six hours of work a day, and it wasn't really hard work. The rest of the time we were free to do whatever we wanted. A few men got into drugs. Yes, we had drugs back then. Have you ever heard of an opium den? That's a place where you go, pay some money, and get high smoking opium. Chinese people ran the dens, I think. I heard they weren't above selling a little dope and taking the rest of your money out of your pocket while you were out there in dreamland. Not too many fellows went to the dens, but I knew of a few. Once a man got started smoking opium, it seemed like he couldn't quit. A lot of soldiers either gambled their pay checks away or spent them on easy women. I sent most of my pay home to Mama and the kids. So, I didn't have the money to fall into the temptations that were all around. Besides, I knew my Papa would turn over in his grave to think one of his boys would behave like hadn't been listening in Sunday school. Papa never had anything to do with gambling, drinking, or women other than Mama. He was a strong Christian man.

I thought Hawaii was the most beautiful place I'd ever seen. Somewhere around here I have some pictures I took back then. You wouldn't believe how things have changed. There's one picture of Diamond Head, taken when I was standing on the beach at Waikiki. Can you imagine? There's not one hotel in sight. Just open country, a sandy beach, and palm trees.

I had never heard of Pearl Harbor before—remember, this was in the early 1920s—but it was easy to see how it got its name. The port area was like a little gem sitting on the bigger jewel of the island of Oahu. People living on the plains had never heard of such a thing as cooling houses with air conditioning. After farming and cow punching outside through the blistering heat and freezing cold, I have to tell you the weather in Hawaii was like something out of a dream.

The plants and flowers were unbelievable. You see post cards of places around the world, and those pictures make everything look so bright and beautiful. Then, when you get to the places where the cards are from, you find out most of the pictures have been retouched. Or maybe there's one city block that looks like the post cards and the rest of the place is completely ordinary. Hawaii never disappoints you that way. Everywhere you look there's something that would make a pretty picture. Sandy beaches, waterfalls, tropical flowers that bloom all year. There's usually a light breeze blowing. Sometimes there's a heavy rain, but most of the moisture comes down in little sprinkly drops that cool things off and barely get you wet. I do think Heaven must be a lot like Hawaii. Or maybe I have that backwards, and Hawaii is a lot like Heaven. I don't see how a place could be any better, I mean as a physical environment, than Hawaii was before World War II.

You may think this is funny, but I'll always remember how good Hawaii smells. There are places in the Pacific that look pretty but stink like a sewer. Hawaii smells like flowers, at least it did when I was there. It's kind of like the honeysuckle we have here in Texas. I can still remember how sweet that air would smell, particularly first thing in the morning and about dusk. There's nothing like it anywhere else I've ever been.

I had one very strange experience in the Islands. That was long before Hawaii became a state, and Honolulu was a wide-open town. Lots of things went on in the territory that they probably wouldn't put up with now.

I remember being downtown Honolulu by myself one afternoon and lo and behold here came somebody I knew walking down the street. This was not a fellow you would want to run into anywhere. He had left Texas after killing another man. Stabbed him to death over a silly little argument. I'd heard about him now and then after that. The story was that he'd gone to New York and become a real thug, working for the mob. Since none of my buddies were with me, I decided I would just walk right by him and hope he wouldn't recognize me in my uniform. It didn't go that way. Just as we started to pass each other on the sidewalk, he grabbed me and threw me up against a wall. "Carl Yeary!" he said in a mean voice. "Do you know who I am?"

Now, if he had walked up and asked me that question, I might have just blurted out the answer, because I did recognize him immediately. By the time I caught my breath, I knew how I had to answer him. "No, sir, I don't believe I know you." I careful-like let my eyes wander left and right, looking for somebody else in uniform or a policeman, or anyone who might respond if I had to holler for help.

"You ever tell anybody you saw me here, I'll kill you. Your family, too," he said. "Swear to me you ain't never going to tell."

"I swear it," I said.

He stared at me some more. I believe he was deciding whether he should let me go or stick a knife in me. As far as I know, I had never done anything to offend this man. I guess he didn't want anybody to find out where he was. If we had met in an alley or somewhere without a lot of people around, I'm certain the Army would have shipped me home in a pine box.

All of a sudden, he turned me loose and went on down the street. I got back to the barracks as fast as I could and didn't leave the post for weeks. It has been more than sixty years since that day, but I still remember the look in that man's eyes. This is the first time I've breathed a word about that encounter to anybody, and I have no intention of telling you his name. He's probably dead by now, but you never know. Besides, I gave him my word. It's bad enough I lied to him and said I didn't know who he was when I really did. No point making it worse by breaking my promise.

So, anyway, instead of spending my time and money on women or getting drunk, I played baseball. We had a team that played every afternoon after work. We played five days a week, and sometimes on the weekend too. I got right into the rhythm of island life, standing guard in the morning and playing baseball in the afternoon. Now and then I would send a post card or a letter to Lucille back in Lake Victor, but I never asked her to be my girl. I did send her a grass hula skirt one time. She wrote back and let me know in no uncertain terms a hula skirt was not an appropriate gift for a young lady. I just thought it was a nice souvenir.

All the time I was in Hawaii, I thought, man this is a good life. But it wasn't long before all that came to an end. One day I got a message to report to the Adjutant's office. When I got there, I was shocked to learn I was being discharged from the Army. Mama had written a letter to some Army brass and told them she needed me back home to run the farm. To this day, I don't know for certain why she did it. I can't imagine she expected me to do any farming. I could never make enough crops to match what the Army paid me. I think maybe it was because she was worried I would lose a prisoner and have to finish up his time in the stockade or even at the Federal prison at Fort Leavenworth. I never should have told Mama about that rule. More likely, she just couldn't stand for one of her kids to be across the ocean from her and the rest of the family.

I didn't want to leave Hawaii, and I sure didn't want to leave the Army. But the decision was already made and I couldn't find any way around it. Altogether I spent about a year and a half in Hawaii. I thought I could have been happy there for the rest of my life, playing baseball and keeping prisoners locked up tight. I was sent back to the west end of Angel Island. I was there a couple of days before they discharged me and put me on a train back to Morton, Texas.

Chapter 12: Surprise, Surprise

Life is full of surprises. When you think you've seen and heard it all, hang on. The next bombshell is probably just around the corner, sitting there waiting to explode in your face. The last thing in the world I expected when I got back to Morton was that Mama was fixing to get married again. I considered myself to be the head of the family after Papa died, but Mama hadn't even talked to me about this thing. I guess Mr. O'Pry was a decent enough fellow, but I never liked him. People told me I would see this differently when I got older, but I've never changed my mind about the situation. Nobody had the right to take my Papa's place. Of course, Mama was never one to listen to reason after she had her mind made up, and she was dead set on marrying Mr. O'Pry.

I'm not sure exactly where Mr. O'Pry was from. Some folks might think of him as citified, or even sissified. He had moved to the Southwest part of the country because he had tuberculosis. In those days, there wasn't any medical treatment for TB, which we also called consumption. People had found they sometimes got better in dry climates like West Texas and New Mexico. It worked for Mr. O'Pry. He got over his illness. He had political connections, too. There was a Texas state senator who was close friends with Mr. O'Pry for their whole lives. It was generally assumed that Mr. O'Pry got his job with the post office because of political influence.

I always had a nagging feeling Mr. O'Pry pulled some strings to get me discharged from the Army, although I never had any proof. After I got home, he told me he could get me an appointment to West Point military academy if I wanted to go. With his friend in the legislature, he probably could have made good on that offer. I turned him down cold. Not that it wasn't a good opportunity, but I never wanted to take one thing from that man, and as far as I know I never did.

After I got back home, I worked around our place for a while, doing things Mama wanted done. Then I went back to work cowboying for Lee Cooper. I worked for him off and on for a while and then came home and helped Ralph and Mama gather the fall crop. Then I went back to work for Old Lee again. I worked for him until 1926.

I wasn't sure what I was going to do next. The only thing that was absolutely certain was that I would never live at home again. I had no plans ever to put my feet under Mr. O'Pry's table. I didn't want to farm, and I wasn't too keen on going back to the cowboy way of life.

A good saddle was a cowboy's most important possession. You spent all day every day sitting on that saddle. If he got rid of his saddle, you knew for sure a cowboy was getting out of the business for good. Well, in 1926, I sold my saddle. You see, I had started to think about getting married. I knew if I had a wife, I'd need to do work where I could come home at night.

After I quit Lee, I went up to New Mexico to work on the wheat harvest. They had a good wheat crop that year up around Clovis. I ended up working for the same guy the whole time I was there. I went down to the grain elevator to ask about a job. I asked this fellow if he knew anybody that was hiring. He said, "Well, I got two or three days work."

I said, "Okay, I'll take it and then I'll look for something after that."

He was threshing his own wheat. He even had his own threshing machine and he traveled around threshing all around the country. Usually his boy drove the truck, hauling wheat. His son was about my age, maybe a couple of years older. After I worked for a couple of days, he said, "I'm going to buy another truck. If you want to drive the old truck, I'll let you do that." So, I went to hauling wheat in the old truck.

Naturally, his boy got the new truck. It had a Ruckstell axle and all that. So, he'd take this Ruckstell axle and cut the first tracks in the field. And that way, I could get out there with his old junker I was driving. But once you got it on the road, it run as good as any of them. So, for a month or two that's all I did, haul wheat out to Greer and Clovis and all around there. And, boy, they were making a lot of wheat out there that year. About sixty bushels an acre, and that's an awful good wheat crop.

I figured it was about this time I quit living day to day and started thinking in terms of the future. I got a steady job working for the railroad. Railroads were big business back then, just about the most reliable employer around. I had to move to Lehman, Texas, which suited me just fine. I wasn't across the ocean from Mama and the kids, but I wouldn't have to hear everybody call Mama "Mrs. O'Pry" all the time either.

After I got a steady job I thought about writing and asking Lucille to marry me, but that didn't seem like the right thing to do. I decided to go back home to Lake Victor and ask her in person. I used to see your grandmother in church back when Papa was alive and we lived in Lake Victor. You couldn't help but notice her, with those big black-brown eyes and shiny black hair. You could see a mile off she was part Indian. I guess you say Native American now, but we said Indian. She was real proud of her Indian blood, which was Osage, part of the Blackfoot nation. You couldn't call her "squaw" though. She didn't like that nickname.

Well, like I said, life sure takes a lot of twists and turns. The first thing I noticed when I saw Lucille was that she was wearing an engagement ring, a big flashy red ruby. I guess that ruby stone was supposed to be kind of cute since her name was Ruby Lucille. Nobody ever called her Ruby, though. It was always Lucille or Lucy up until you renamed her Bango. Now I had never made her any promises or asked her to wait for me. So I didn't have any right to be upset that she went and got engaged, but I went right ahead and got riled up anyway. That fellow Andy she was planning to marry was not near good enough for her in my estimation.

Chapter 13: Wedding Bells

That's the best thing I ever did, marrying Lucille. Her father died in the Spanish flu epidemic, just like Papa did. Her mother was left a widow with four children. Lucille was the oldest one, probably about ten or eleven.

Belle, her mother, was left a widow with four kids. Back then, there wasn't any social security or welfare to help out widows. Widow women just did whatever they could to put food on the table. I thought we had it hard in our family, but at least we had a little land. Belle sold homemade bread and took in laundry.

Laundry in them days wasn't just a matter of putting loads of clothes in a fancy washer and dryer like you do now. Belle and Bango had to build a fire in the back yard and heat up a big metal washtub of water to wash clothes. They used lye soap and agitated the clothes by stirring them in the tub with broomsticks. Back then, we thought things like men's shirts ought to be stiffened up with starch to give them character. That meant taking the shirts after they were washed and rinsed and wrung out and dipping them in another cauldron of hot starch solution. Then they hung everything outside on the clothesline to dry.

Washing wasn't the worst of it. After the clothes dried, they had to bring them in and iron them. The irons were heavy hunks of metal with a wooden handle. You heated them on the wood stove. Most time when you'd see a woman ironing, she'd have at least two irons going. One would sit on the stove heating up while she ironed with the other one. When the iron she was using cooled off too much to do any good, she'd put it on the stove, take up the other iron and go to town again. Try it sometime. Try ironing a starched shirt collar with a flat iron without scorching it and without leaving any wrinkles in it. It's not that easy. Of course, if you scorched something, you had to wash it again and start all over.

After a while, Belle was lucky enough to get the job of operating the switchboard for the telephone company. That switchboard was a fascinating piece of equipment. Lucille could operate it as good as Belle, and a good deal of the time she did. The operator had to plug cord in to the right spot to complete the call. It was an ancestor of the modern PBX. The only drawback to being the town telephone operator was that you had to be available all the time to put calls through. Still, it beat taking in laundry by a country mile.

Belle found herself another husband before Lucille and I married. Mr. Jackson was a widower with a couple of kids. Her four, his two, and then they had another baby together, Emmitt. Belle just took care of all of them. There never was a finer woman walked on this earth than Belle Jackson. She had as hard a life as anybody, and I never one time ever heard her complain about it.

Well, to get back to my story, I still don't know exactly how but in pretty short order I convinced Lucille to break off her engagement and marry me instead of Old Andy. I went down to Lampasas and Lucille and I got married on the fifth of August, 1926. We moved out to Lehman and set up housekeeping in two rooms and a bath. Lehman wasn't much of a town. The name of the railroad that ran by it was the South Plains and Santa Fe, and its general manager was Mr. Frank Lehman. So I guess you can figure out how the place got its name. The only reason for the town's existence was the railroad that transported cattle to market from the ranches around that area. There were a few houses, a school, and some businesses. Naturally, you had to have a café where cowboys could get something to eat when they brought a herd in. Once in a while I would run into some of the wranglers I had worked with before I went in the Army.

We were poor as Job's turkey, but we didn't know that. We were as happy as any two people could be. In 1927 our little girl was born there in Lehman. If we'd had a boy, Lucille wanted to name him William for me and her brother. When the baby turned out to be a girl, Lucille just would name her Billie. She said if she spelled it "Billie" instead of "Billy" then it became a girl's name, but I never was convinced.

I got to calling the baby by her middle name of Louise and after a while Lucille gave in and called her Louise, too. After she got grown, my daughter preferred to be called Billie. I've always called her Louise, though. That's a girl's name. Lucille and I were both crazy about little Louise. You might think I'm only saying this because she's my daughter, but Louise was the smartest kid I ever saw.

Northing would irritate my wife more than for somebody to say how cute Louise was and then ask who she belonged to. Both our kids had blond hair and blue eyes. They just looked just like all the other Yearys. Bango with her dark hair and eyes and Louise with her cotton top never did look like mother and daughter. Lucille and her brothers and sisters got their dark looks from her father. Her mother, Belle, was a blue-eyed blond.

My job at the railroad seemed secure, but out of the blue they decided to close down the Lehman depot. I think they even tore down the building after we left town. I don't know why. Maybe the materials were going to be used to build another depot somewhere else. We made up a little ditty about it:

> The train don't stop in Lehman town
> 'Cause the woodpeckers pecked the depot down.

I started looking for another job as soon as I heard talk about the railroad leaving Lehman. I ran into somebody who worked for Lee Cooper, a man I had worked for in the past, and asked if anybody was hiring cowboys. Old Lee said he would give me some work when he could. I could see he didn't really need another hand. He was just willing to help me out for old times' sake. I always appreciated Lee for that kindness, but it bothered me, too. It felt like taking charity.

I didn't want to go back to being a cowboy for a long stretch anyway. Lucille and I had a toddler and another baby on the way. I had got spoiled to eating supper with my family and being at home with them of an evening.

Chapter 14: Riding the Rails

Along in the spring, it got dry and Lee didn't have anything to do and he laid me off. A man gets real low when he can't find any work, especially if he has a wife and family depending on him. So, I got kind of desperate and decided to ride the rails and find work somewhere else. Needless to say, we didn't have the money for me to buy a ticket.

Riding the rails means sneaking aboard a train and getting a free ride. It was dangerous business in the twenties and thirties. Railroad men would shoot people in those days if they caught them riding the rails. I figured I knew enough about how the railroad worked to get by with it. Most of us when we're young think we're stronger and smarter than we really are.

You would never want to try to sneak onto a train in town. There are too many railroad men around, what we called "bulls". They had shotguns and most of the time there weren't any questions asked when they used them. At least that's how it was back during the depression. So, you stay out of sight and walk out of town far enough to avoid the bulls, but close enough to get on the train before it picks up too much speed. Freight trains are the best transportation because they don't stop as often as passenger trains. Also, you don't have people looking out of windows and maybe spotting you.

I've heard it said the people who had money to buy tickets to ride called us bums and freeloaders. I can understand their point of view. On the other hand, I couldn't see that we were hurting anybody. The trains were going to run whether a few of us bums got a ride or not. I can't tell you whether all the railroad men and paying customers looked down on freeloaders or just a few.

Some of the men I met while riding the rails had become professional hobos, just drifting from one place to another without any hope of ever going back to a normal family life. Too many of those hobos wanted nothing more than the money to buy enough whiskey to get drunk.

Occasionally you'd run into some old boy who had his guitar or harmonica with him. When you were away from town and the bulls, these musicians would pass the time singing songs about good days in the past or better days to come. One of the songs I remember was "Big Rock Candy Mountain." I never could sing worth a hoot myself.

For the most part, the bums were pretty nice guys. Oh, once in a while you'd run into some old sourpuss who hated the world or tried to gyp you out of your clothes or steal your shoes. The majority of the men I ran into were just like me, down on their luck and trying to get to some place where they could make a living. Most of them would share their food with you if they had any.

Here and there I would pick up a few days of manual labor, enough to keep me going but not enough to do any good. The whole country was having hard times. I went across New Mexico and Arizona, all the way to California. When I couldn't find steady work there, I decided it was time to give up and go back to Texas. I was mighty lonesome for Lucille and the kids. The closer I got to home, the less I wanted to stop and look for work. I just wanted to be back with my family. Somewhere along the way I figured I could make the rest of the trip without stopping if I only ate a meal every other day.

I was walking by the tracks when a guy come along in a Model T Ford and wanted to know if I wanted a ride. I said, "Sure. I appreciate every mile you can get me down to road toward home." He said he was just going a little ways out in the country. We went on out there fifteen or twenty miles. He turned across the railroad tracks and told me he that was as far as he was going in my direction. From there on, he was heading south.

There was a little old flag station and a small depot at the place where he crossed the tracks. From my experience working for the railroad, I knew only passenger trains would be stopping there. But I thought maybe a freight train would go by slow enough that I might be able to catch it when it came through.

I wasn't there but a little bit until a passenger train come in, heading the way I wanted to go. I said, well, I've never blinded a passenger train, but here's where we start. I figured I had to get on the opposite side of the track from the depot, on the north side, so they wouldn't see me. So, I walked around the train and waited until I thought nobody was looking. Then I hopped up on what they call the blinds, the space between the coal car, right behind the engine, and the coach or the baggage car. I made it onto the train.

I knew the next town coming up, Fort Sumner, was on the same side of the train I was on. I figured I had to get on the other side of the train somehow if I didn't want them to see me when they pulled in there. So, I climbed up on top of the train, right there in broad daylight, hoping the engineer and fireman wouldn't see me. I walked over the top of that moving train and got into the other side of the blind so I would be hidden from the railroad people when we got to Fort Sumner.

We weren't at Fort Sumner very long. When we pulled out, I knew the train wasn't going to stop any more until we got to Clovis. So I felt pretty good then. They had some good trains out there then, the Santa Fe did. This one was a good, fast train.

I was real happy when I finally crossed the state line going into Texas. I calculated we would be going through a little town not too far from Morton not long after daybreak. I can't think of the name of the town right now, just a small place. The best thing about that town was that it was all on one side of the railroad tracks.

I knew the freight train I was on wasn't going to stop there, but they had to slow down for the crossing where cars drove over the tracks. There probably wouldn't be as many bulls in a small place, either. I was planning on jumping off the side away from town just before we got to the crossing. Then I would walk on in to town and spend the two dimes I had left on a good enough breakfast to make the walk over to Morton. I don't know exactly how far it was, less than thirty miles.

As we got close to town, I eased out on the side of the train and looked for a good spot to jump off. I made a mistake, though. What I thought was level ground was really deep ravine, but I saw that too late to keep from jumping. As soon as I let go, I went tumbling down into that ravine. I sat there at the bottom for a while, kind of stunned. I was banged up, with a few bruises and all, but no bones were broken.

I walked the couple of miles into town, feeling every step. When I was a young man, it didn't take me as long to get sore as it does now. Anyhow, when I got to the café, I put my hand in my pocket and it was empty. I couldn't believe it. I kept going through different pockets looking for them two dimes I had been saving to get something to eat. Finally, I figured out the money must have fallen out when I fell down into that ravine. I thought for a minute about going back out there, but the chances of finding the exact spot where I jumped off the train and then finding where the coins fell out was just about nil.

I walked on by the café and headed out towards Morton. Along about noon I was so hungry I didn't think I could go on. I saw a farmhouse sitting back off the road and decided I would go ask for a handout. From time to time, people would knock on the door and ask for something to eat where we lived in Lehman, but I had never done anything like that myself. I was glad Lucille had never turned those men down. She was thrifty, but she wasn't stingy. All the time I was getting over to that farm house, I was hoping the people that lived there would have a soft heart like my wife's.

I went to the back of the farm house and knocked on the door. I guess you know beggars don't go to the front door. I didn't mean to tell my life story to the woman who came to the door, but I wasn't thinking all that straight. I told her about looking for work and riding the rails and losing my two dimes.

She said, "Wait here." In a little while that lady brought me a big, fat sandwich and a tall glass of cold buttermilk. I've never had a meal in my life that tasted as good as that one. I had no way to show my appreciation, other than to say thank you. So, I did that and went on to my brother Ralph's place in Morton.

I never knew her name, but to my way of thinking that farmer's wife was an angel.

Chapter 15: San Angelo

One day my brother-in-law, Clarence, came by to see us. You know Clarence, Lucille's younger brother. He had worked in the oil fields for a while, but was looking around for something better. He said he was headed to San Angelo, where he'd heard there was a lot of work available. Clarence said San Angelo was booming, getting to be a real prosperous place.

The idea of a big town sounded real good to Lucille and me after living in Lehman where there wasn't anything much at all. We talked it over and decided we would move down there. So we packed up the baby and our few belongings in a Model T Ford and headed for the big city of San Angelo. We were in for a rough time regardless of where we went, but we didn't know that yet. It was late summer, 1929.

Work wasn't as available in San Angelo as Clarence had heard, although that may have been a matter of timing. When we headed to San Angelo, Lucille's brother decided he would go with us. So, there we were, Don and Clarence and Lucille and the baby and me. None of us had enough money to shake a stick at. When we got into San Angelo, I managed to rent us a motel room, right there by the depot. Well, I went out the next day and got me a job. Then I got busy looking for a place to live.

Don and Clarence hung around two or three more days and still hadn't found any work. One day a guy come out to the tourist court where we were staying and asked if there was anybody who wanted to work on a bridge gang. If I had been there, I would have gone to work on that bridge gang. But the train was leaving and the guy had to have somebody right away. So, he hired Clarence and Don. They went out to Fort Stockton, or somewhere out that way, wherever the bridge was. Don worked till he got enough money to go home and then that's what he did. He went home. But Lucille's brother Clarence stayed there for about a year and worked on that bridge gang. He was making more money than I was.

I got on as a swamper with the San Angelo Transfer Company. That was a local trucking company that operated in and around San Angelo. It didn't pay a lot, but I figured I would move on to something better as soon as we got settled. What does a swamper do? Well, I rode in the back of a big truck. When the truck stopped, I loaded cargo and then unloaded it when we got to the warehouse. If the floor needed sweeping, I'd sweep it. If something broke down, I'd do my best to fix it or help someone else fix it. I'd do whatever I could find to make myself useful.

Eventually I got to work in the warehouse checking stuff out of cars. We had what we called pool cars there. Inventory would come in from different wholesale houses and we would unload and haul their products, or store them in the warehouse until they wanted to come get them.

They were pretty good to us at the transfer company. By then Lucille and I had two kids, our daughter Louise and a son we named Leon. His first name was Carl, but since that's my name too, we called him by his middle name. At Christmas, Old Man Frank Van Court gave every employee of the transfer company a turkey and a big basket of fruit and candy for their kids.

After I started working at the transfer company, Lucille decided we needed to buy a house so we could quit paying rent. She always felt like rent was a waste of money, and you know how she hated to waste anything. We looked around and found a nice house for sale there in San Angelo. The payments were going to come to two dollars and fifty cents a week, and I couldn't see any way we could afford to pay that much. I put pencil to paper and figured every which way. There just wasn't enough money to take care of the kids and pay the bills and buy a house.

There's one thing I didn't fully realize about Lucille until after we were married. I thought I had learned to be very careful about spending money. She made me look like an amateur in that department. Lucille could squeeze a nickel until the buffalo begged for mercy. Back then, all of the nickels had a buffalo on one side. I don't care how tight things got or how little we had, my wife always put aside something out of every week's wages. She said she was saving up for a rainy day.

Well, she told me if I'd get the loan to buy the house, she'd make the budget work somehow. And that's what we did. I don't know how she stretched out my paycheck to cover everything, probably by doing without things she needed. But we got the house she wanted on Perry Street and we lived there for a number of years.

Now you're too young to remember this, but if you read up on your history, you'll realize the whole financial structure of the United States collapsed in the fall of 1929. At first it was just the stock market, but the problem fanned out to affect almost everybody. Texas was in pretty good shape for a while, until the price of cotton hit rock bottom.

Not long after Leon was born, Old Man Frank Van Court called all of the employees of the Transfer Company together. We knew it wasn't going to be good news because banks were failing left and right, business were closing down, and people were getting laid off in droves. Mr. Van Court told us the way things were going he couldn't stay afloat and keep all of us on the payroll full time. He said he was considering two options. One was to let most of us go. The alternative was to keep everybody employed for the time being and spread the work out so nobody would get to work every day but everybody would get to work some.

Then he surprised us by saying he thought the only fair way to decide this thing was to put it to a vote. There was no union involved. Whatever decisions Old Man Frank made, we would have had to accept. He didn't have to let us have any say, but that's how he wanted to do it.

Each man got one vote, by secret ballot. I didn't have to think this over at all. I expected I would be one of the first to go if they started laying people off. With two kids, one of them a brand new baby, and a wife to support, I was sure hoping the vote would go my way. Old Man Frank took up the votes and went upstairs to the office. We were in a big, open warehouse with a wooden staircase against one side leading up to the office, which was like a wooden box sitting on an elevated platform. There was a big window in side of the office so whoever was in there could look out and see all around the warehouse.

While Mr. Van Court was up there counting votes, I was thinking what I would do if I lost my job. I didn't think the Army would take me back now that I had a family. I didn't have any land to farm and no way of getting any. The only other thing I knew was cowboying. I worried about where Lucille and the kids could stay if I went back on the trail.

Old Man Frank came down and told us we were all going to stay, and everybody cheered. He made it clear he would determine who worked, when, and how often, and he didn't want to hear any griping about his decisions. Things were pretty rough for a year or so. I generally worked a day or two a week.

Like most towns of any size back then, San Angelo had a vacant lot where men would go and wait for casual work. For example, if a farmer needed the weeds chopped out of a field, he would come by the vacant lot and pick out some men to work for a couple of days to take care of that chore. I spent a lot of days standing in that vacant lot. Some days I would get work, and more often I would not. It's a good thing Lucille was smart enough to put aside a little money while I worked for the railroad. It's also a good thing she kept our savings in a Folgers coffee can instead of putting it in the bank.

As I said, I generally got a day or two a week at the Transfer Company along with whatever odd jobs I could pick up. Sure, those were hard times, but that's all life had been for me since Papa died, except for that that brief stint in the Army. When Papa told me, "When you go out to face the world in the morning, you better have your fighting britches on," he was right. Taking care of my wife and kids was a struggle. On the other hand, the four of us had each other. And that was enough.

A few employees left the Transfer Company for better jobs, or left town hoping to find something better. I might have done the same thing if I had thought there was any possibility of bettering my situation. Lucille and I kept the kids fed and clothed and a roof over our heads, and that was about it. We did without a lot of things, but Lucille never complained. I guess she was like her mother Belle that way.

Chapter 16: In Sickness and In Health

I sent off for a correspondence course in double entry bookkeeping. I must have learned what I needed to know because the transfer company's books balanced out at the end of every month. Lucille and I weren't wealthy, but after I started keeping books we could give Louise and Leon each a dime to go to the movies on Saturday. Admission was a nickel, and the rest was for popcorn or candy. Our kids had enough food and decent clothes to wear to school. We even bought a real nice radio.

I worked in the office for the same wages I got in the warehouse for a little while. Then they must have decided I could handle things and I went from eighteen dollars a week up to twenty-five dollars a week, which was a big jump for me.

For entertainment, we sat on the porch after supper and visited with the neighbors. They were all just as poor as we were, so we had a lot in common. Lucille always made lots of friends wherever she went. She loved being with other people, even those I thought were too ornery to put up with. Emmitt and Lucy Sheffield were our closest friends, though. Emmitt could make a wooden Indian laugh. Our kids were about the same age and played together.

Lucille and I loved that house. It's where we raised our children. It meant something that we owned the place instead of being renters, too. That gave us a sense of permanence, you know? Along with the house, we gained entry into a close-knit community of neighbors.

Back then, you knew your neighbors. Nowadays, people turn on the air conditioner, close their windows, and shut out the rest of the world. It was too hot for us to keep our windows closed in the summertime, which in San Angelo could go from March through November. We knew whether or not families yelled at each other and what kind of music they listened to on the radio because we could hear it going on. Buying that house put us in the middle of some real good neighbors.

Little by little things eased up. Which is to say, I was able to get more days of work. Then Lucille got sick. The doctors said she had a tubal pregnancy that had burst. When they did surgery, they told me she had peritonitis and they didn't think she was going to live. She told me later she fought to hold on because she couldn't stand the thought of somebody else raising her children.

When she finally came home from the hospital, Lucille she was so weak she couldn't get out of bed. Leon was still a toddler and Louise wasn't old enough to go to school yet. When I got a chance to work, I had to go. So, Lucy Sheffield looked after the kids. They played with her kids and she fed them and kept them out of the house so Lucille could rest until I got home in the evening. Very often I would leave for work in the morning and come home to find the laundry done and some food in the oven, not even knowing for sure which neighbor woman was responsible. If it hadn't been for our neighbors, I don't see how we would have made it. Emmitt and Lucy Sheffield were two of the finest people I ever knew.

I guess everybody had it pretty rough during the thirties. People lost a lot of money. Lucille and I didn't have any to lose. She'd always been poor, and I had got used to it after Papa died. So, we really didn't notice that much difference before or after what they called 'the crash" in 1929. One thing you can be sure of. All of our married life, no matter how much or how little I made, Lucille would put some of it away for a rainy day. And all the way through the Depression, we never missed a payment on our house.

The doctors told Bango she would never have another child. I think she grieved some over that because she really loved babies. When my brother Calaway died and orphaned three little girls, Lucille took those kids in and loved them right along with ours. We were all disappointed when the girls left us. The family decided they should be raised by some more prosperous relatives. I can't argue that point, but nobody would ever have been a better mother to those kids than Lucille.

I started playing baseball with a local semi-pro team. That doesn't mean I made any money. Don't your eyes bug out when you hear the kind of salaries athletes make today? Back then being semi-pro meant you didn't have to pay for your uniform or equipment. Some local establishment, like maybe a grocery store, would buy a team's uniforms for the privilege of putting their name on the backs of the shirts. Lucille never cared anything about sports, but she brought Leon and Louise to my home games anyway.

Of course, Louise loved for me to take her to the library. A lot of Sunday afternoons, the four of us would go out to the Ben Ficklin Reservoir and fish or swim. After I started working in the warehouse office and got a raise, we could afford to give the kids a dime each to go to the movies on Saturday. Everything considered, those years in San Angelo were real good ones.

Chapter 17: Goodfellow

Radio was becoming a big thing in this country in the late 1920s. Nowadays if somebody wants something they go down to the store and get it, even if they have to buy it on credit. The whole way of thinking was different then. After some investigation, I found out I could order a kit and build my own radio. As soon as Lucille decided we could afford it, I sent off for the kit. It wasn't a pretty thing. In fact it was kind of crazy looking, just some wires, a coil, a crystal and a set of earphones. That crystal was very temperamental and often had more static than people would put up with now, but to us that radio was amazing. It brought in information about the whole country, the whole world in fact. As soon as something happened, somebody would get on the air and tell all about it. I thought radio was a great invention and was going to be the coming thing. Building that radio was one of the most interesting things I'd ever done.

Speaking of radio, that was the cause of the only serious argument Lucille and I had in almost seventy years of marriage. It was over politics. In 1938 W. Lee O'Daniel ran for governor of Texas. As far as I was concerned, he was a radio personality and wasn't qualified to run the state. They called him "Pappy" Lee O'Daniel or "Pass the Biscuits" O'Daniel on the air. Bob Wills played music on O'Daniel's program. You probably never heard of the Light Crust Dough Boys, but they were a musical sensation in the thirties, at least in Texas they were.

We were talking about the election one evening, sitting on the porch. I couldn't believe my ears when Lucille said she was going to vote for Pappy O'Daniel for governor. Right away I asked her why. She said it was because she liked the music on his radio show. I told her that was no reason to vote for him to be the governor of the State of Texas, but she wouldn't budge. We argued with each other the whole evening. She didn't have one good reason to vote for that man.

Of course, I cancelled out her vote with mine, but O'Daniel won anyway. I can't say he was the worst governor we ever had. There's a lot of competition for that title. But the right to vote is serious business and it made me mad that Lucille would throw her vote away foolishly. It was a subject we could never discuss because both of us would get mad all over again if we did. To tell you the truth, I'm a little agitated right now just thinking about her wasting her vote on that stinking O'Daniel.

That correspondence course I took in bookkeeping taught me something besides how to figure. It showed me I could learn things from books. The course I took, along with the practical application of keeping ledgers, made me start believing I might be able to learn something more. Maybe I could move up in the world some more. I was always interested in radio and electronics. That first crystal set I built from a kit gave me a basic understanding of connecting wires and making things work. I continued to tinker around, fixing ours and the neighbors' radios when they went on the blink.

One day I saw an advertisement in a Popular Mechanics magazine for the Chicago Institute of Engineering that offered a variety of courses by correspondence. Right away I was interested. Not knowing whether or not it would ever lead to anything, I signed up for a course that dealt with radio. I kept on going, taking different subjects until finally I graduated. There's a framed diploma around here somewhere from the Chicago Institute. I studied hard because I really enjoyed learning about electricity and radio transmission, things like that.

I met up with some fellows with similar interests and got into ham radio. Do you know what that is? Well, it's a national network of amateur radio operators. For me it was a hobby, something to do while Lucille was playing cards or dominoes with the neighbors. She loved to play games but I never saw any sense to it myself. Hams communicate with each other to keep in practice. They can provide a valuable service when there's a natural disaster. When a flood or tornado hits, normal communications are disrupted. Hams can get on the air and let people know what happened and to send help. I learned Morse code so I could send messages that way.

Some of the other hams started talking to me about going to work at Goodfellow Field in San Angelo. It's Goodfellow Air Force Base now, but back then there wasn't any such thing as the Air Force. The Air Corps was part of the Army. Anyhow, these old boys finally convinced me to apply for a civil service job teaching electronics to soldiers out at the air base. It was a different kind of thing, teaching was. I studied hard to know the material well enough to explain it and answer questions. That was a real good job. It paid well, and I always enjoyed being in a military environment. So, my hobby and my work got all mixed up together. That suited me just fine. I taught electronics during the day and fooled around with radio equipment on my own time.

My ham buddies put another idea in my head. They were members of the naval reserve outfit. That meant they had to go to reserve meetings once in a while and participate in drills. The benefit was that they got cast-off parts the Navy didn't need any more. The idea of free electronic gear got my attention right away. I was kind of old to be joining up, in my mid-thirties, but that didn't appear to be any obstacle. Since I had previously been in the Army, the Naval Reserves took me right in. Sure enough, I was able to get all the surplus tubes and wires and things I could use. They might not have been the latest invention, but I was happy to have them.

The Great Depression had knocked our little family for a loop, and I'd almost lost my wife to a serious illness. By 1940, we were back on our feet. Lucille and I had our own house and an automobile. Louise and Leon were growing up to be fine kids. Everybody was healthy. One thing I've learned about life is this: when things start going along pretty smooth, you better watch your backside. Something may be creeping up on you.

Chapter 18: This Means War

Lucille and her whole family were members of the Church of Christ. Since we didn't have one near us in San Angelo, we sent our kids to Sunday school at the Baptist church in our neighborhood. I guess the right thing would have been to take the kids ourselves, but we seldom did that. That must be how Louise ended up being a life-long Baptist. On Sunday mornings, after we got the kids off to Sunday school, Lucille and I would listen to the radio and read the paper and have a leisurely morning. After Sunday dinner, we would take the kids out to the dam on the Ben Ficklin River. We would wade or fish or just walk around out there in the country.

The news in the early 1940s sometimes mentioned the mess that was festering over in Europe. Most Americans at that time figured we would sit this one out. A lot of people still remembered World War I and we didn't have the stomach for another fight. The naval reserve unit I belonged to gave no indication of getting ready for anything special. To tell you the truth it was more like a social club than a military organization.

All that changed on December 7, 1941. Louise and Leon had just come in from church, and Lucille was putting food on the table for lunch. When I heard that the Japanese had bombed Pearl Harbor, I said, "That means war!" I guess I hollered that out, because everybody came running. The four of us sat there glued to that radio. After a while, the men in the neighborhood got together and talked about what was going to happen. It was like you flipped a light switch on, the change in everybody's attitude. On Saturday night nobody in our neighborhood was too interested in that European fracas. By Sunday afternoon, it was personal. The only decision the young men had to make was Army, Navy, or Marines.

I did a lot of thinking right about then. I guess we all did. I was creeping up on forty years old, with a wife and two kids. I didn't want to go off and leave my family, but nobody else did either. Louise was about the age I was when Papa died. Leon was even younger. I didn't want them to finish growing up without a father. On the other hand, I was worried about the kind of world they were going to inherit if somebody didn't go whip the Japs and Germans.

The only reason I was a reservist was because I was either cheap or greedy, whatever you want to call it, to get free radio parts. But the fact of the matter was, right down at the core I knew I wanted to go and fight. When I went to bed on the night of December 7th, I was glad I had joined the naval reserves. That meant I didn't have to decide whether or not to enlist, and I didn't have to explain myself to anybody. Not that Lucille would ever have questioned my decision. It was comfortable knowing I was going to go and fight, no doubt about it.

Now you and your generation look at World War II from this side of the thing, after we won. From the other side, when the war was just starting, we didn't know that. At the time, it wasn't too hard to imagine the Japanese taking Asia, the Germans getting Europe and Africa, and us getting carved up and split between them. Or maybe them whipping everybody else and then turning on each other and slugging it out until one of them ruled the whole world. I never did get to hating our enemies the way some guys did, but I sure didn't want Hitler or Hirohito having any say-so over my kids' lives either.

With all the men scurrying off to war, all of the sudden there was a labor shortage in San Angelo. People were begging for workers. They started hiring women for jobs that up to then had been done by men. Women on farms and ranches around where I grew up always worked hard. So. I never had the idea some men have that it's a shame if his wife had a job. When Lucille told me she felt like she had to do something to support the war, I didn't discourage her.

Lucille took a job working in a laundry. She walked a long way to work, at least three miles, maybe four, and back again in the evening. She hadn't driven a car since before we got rid of our Model T Ford.

You know how your grandmother was. If she met somebody she didn't know, she would strike up a conversation. In a little while they would be telling her their life story or confiding all their troubles. It turned out most of the people who worked in the laundry were deaf. So what did she do? She learned sign language. Good thing, too. Later on, when some dry-cleaning fluid caught on fire, she went through the laundry signing the word f-i-r-e and got everybody out of the building before it burned down.

I didn't worry about getting killed in the war. I knew it was a possibility, but I did my best not to think about. For sure, I never talked about it. Death is just something a man has to be prepared for when he puts on the uniform.

One thing was certain. Nobody was ever going to beat my wife out of what we had while I was gone. Lucille wasn't like Mama. She had a good head for business. She might not know a lot of fancy financial terminology, but she didn't turn loose of a cent without understanding exactly where it was going and why. I can't tell you how many times I heard her tell the kids, "Take care of your pennies, and your dollars will take care of themselves."

Bango didn't show her temper much. One of her favorite sayings was, "Anger improves nothing but the arch in a cat's back." But I learned early on it was possible to make her mad if someone tried hard enough. When somebody finally stepped over the line, those dark eyes would snap and she would set them straight right quick like.

Here's a story I didn't hear until I got home from the war. There was a man who didn't go to war, who liked to throw his weight around with the women and kids in the neighborhood while the men folk were off fighting. He was a big man, loud, no account if you ask me. Anyhow, this old boy got after Leon one day. He came up in our front yard, grabbed Leon, and said he was going to give him a whipping. Leon was always small for his age, and he couldn't have been more than twelve or thirteen when this happened. I don't doubt our son had done something he shouldn't have. Leon could be a rascal. But this man should have come and talked to an adult instead of deciding to take matters into his own hands with a kid half his size.

Lucille was in the house and heard the commotion. She ran outside and saw this man had ahold of Leon, who was screaming his lungs out. She hollered at the man to let Leon go, and he said he would after he gave him a beating. Now, you know she was a little tiny woman. She always claimed to be five feet four inches tall, but she had to fudge to reach that. I don't know where she got the strength, but she picked up a heavy iron lawn chair and laid that man out cold with it. She took Leon in the house and left the neighbor man laying out there unconscious. She said she never did know if somebody came and got him or if he came to on his own.

Lucille would grin when someone brought up this story and add that the bully never bothered Leon again. When I told her she could have killed that man, she said it would have served him right. Like I said, she didn't get riled too often. But when she did, she was mad clean through.

Chapter 19: Shipping Out

I probably would have got a commission in the Army Air Force if I'd stayed on instructing electronics. But, since I was in the naval reserves, the Navy reached out their long arm and put me on active duty before that could happen. I got a parcel post package full of uniforms in a couple of weeks after Pearl Harbor with instructions to report for duty in January, 1942. A lot of men I knew from San Angelo went to Europe. They were mostly in the Army, what we called 'ground pounders'.

When I reported, the Navy sent me to Dallas first of all. In Dallas they put together a bunch of people that had just come in and enlisted. Of course, they found out right away that I'd been in the service before. Since I had prior service and was such an old man, they put me in charge and sent us to New Orleans. We got down there and they processed us through. For a while, they put me to work as a gate guard.

I stood gate guard watches for a few days and then they sent me down to where they were bringing in small ships, PT boats and stuff like that. They were building them up north but they couldn't put the superstructure on them until they got to New Orleans because of some of the low clearance bridges on the Mississippi River. So, they would tow them down the Mississippi to New Orleans and bring them in there and put the superstructure on them, the guns and everything. They'd put a pre-commissioning crew on the ships, shake them down, and turn them over to the permanent crew when they got there.

I stayed in New Orleans until they were ready to send me to school. Anybody who could pass certain tests—and especially if you were an amateur radio operator—they figured you knew something about electronics and they wanted to send you to materiel school. I kind of liked working on the pre-commissioning crew, and I wanted to stay where I was. But that didn't happen.

The Navy sent me to pre-radar school at Oklahoma A&M College, in Stillwater, Oklahoma. I stayed there for several months, going to school. I thought they'd ship me out of there to the west coast or somewhere. Well, somebody came along and started a new program for naval aviation. This school for this was at the Naval Air Station at Ward Island, down near Corpus

Christi, Texas. They had us all fall in one morning. They counted off so many and said, "You people are going to Corpus Christi, Ward Island, to the Naval Aviation Materiel School." So I went down there for another three or four months of school in airborne radar and radio, and stuff like that.

When I was about done with my training at Corpus Christi, they called in ten or twelve of us who had previous service. We thought they were going to send us somewhere to set up another school or something. Instead, they gave us sealed orders and put us on a train. When we got aboard and read our orders, we found out we were going to a Naval Air Station at Sand Point, up near Lake Washington, close to Seattle. Our status was "FFT", which means "for further transfer." We didn't stay at Sand Point very long.

The Navy was in the process of building a naval air station at Whidbey Island. Of course, we didn't know any of this. They loaded us up in a cattle car—they called them busses, but they were more like a cattle car—and hauled us up to Whidbey Island. They hadn't yet commissioned the sea plane base up there. We were the commissioning crew for this base. They brought PBYs and things in, and we started training to go north. A PBY is what a civilian would call a flying boat, an amphibious aircraft.

They recommissioned Fleet Air Wing Six, which had been deactivated for a long time. It was first commissioned in World War I, and shut down shortly thereafter. I got to be a pretty good airborne radar operator there. Nobody knew much about it then. Somebody had to start in. There were two radiomen in each PBY crew, first and second radioman, and one of them would operate the radar. Well, I got to be pretty good at that radar. They put up the first homing station for radar there. Do you know what IFF is? It stands for 'Identification, Friend or Foe'. It's a way to identify aircraft as friendly and get their bearing and range. We kind of jury rigged an IFF, put it on the same frequency we were using, and fixed it so it wouldn't sweep, and the radar would pick it up. We used that for a homing station. They later built radar beacon stations using radar like that.

We trained there at Whidbey Island for a while then went on up north. There, they had swapped territory. When we went up there, Fleet Air Wing 4 was up there and they had the territory from Kodiak Island west, and we were taking over the territory from Kodiak Island back to Tongue Point, Oregon. Then they decided it was time to swap the thing because Fleet Air Wing 4 had been flying this route. So, they put FAW 4 on the Kodiak Island to Tongue Point, Oregon route, and put us on the Kodiak West route. You had to be a good radar operator up there. If you weren't, you were liable to wind up in the icy water. I learned most of my real sharp radar operating from some of them guys who'd been up there before. I'd get them to show me and tell me things.

They came in with an order, to get people to form a new unit, which was a carrier unit. They picked out about 12 people out of the area, not all from FAW 5 or 4, but from different outfits. I happened to be one of them. They sent us to Alameda, California. As soon as they gathered all of the people to form this new unit, they discovered there wasn't enough room to put us all up at Alameda. Then they sent us up north to Santa Rosa where they were building a little air station and had a barracks. We waited there for a ship to come in and pick us up. They ended up putting us on a Dutch ship, and we headed south. The Dutch ship traveled alone. They wouldn't travel in convoy because they had a diesel motor and could travel a lot faster than a convoy. We went along the West Coast to somewhere off South America, and then headed west to Tahiti. From Tahiti we went on across to New Caledonia.

It's funny. I picked up a card in Tahiti and sent it to Lucille. They censored out the unit and all, but the card went through the mail. They might as well have left it alone, because it was obvious where I was. I think that card is still around the house somewhere. You know how Lucille always kept everything.

We went on over to New Caledonia and laid around there for a day or two. Then we got our final orders to the New Hebrides, where we were going to service the carriers. At that time, the carriers would come out of combat back to the New Hebrides to get refueled, serviced, repaired, and in general get ready to go again. We stayed there for a few months and serviced the planes that would come off the carriers. Then they came in and picked us up with another Dutch ship.

The first Dutch ship we were on was the Bloemfontein, out of San Francisco. This one was the Japara. They both had what was known as marifoam bows that would crush through the ice. They would just slide up on it and crush the ice and they could go through it, I guess because there was a lot of ice in the North Sea. Anyway, we went on up to Guadalcanal, which was pretty well secured by then, and put some soldiers off there. I didn't go ashore at Guadalcanal. We went on up past Guadalcanal through the Russell Islands, stopping and putting more people off. Our commanding officer said, "I don't want to keep you people in the dark. I'm going to tell you where we're going. We're going to Beefsteak."

Of course, 'Beefsteak' was a code word, and it didn't mean anything to me. We went on up to Rendova, Munda, the Treasuries, Green, and finally to Emirau. That's where we were headed. The Marines had made the invasion at Emirau, which was about 85 miles from Kavieng. Kavieng and Rabaul were Japanese strongholds. We expected trouble, but never had much trouble at Emirau. The only thing the Japanese had there was a radio station, which the marines took before we came ashore.

The only harbor they had at Emirau had a big cliff around it. It was just back in a cove. After the Marines went ashore and secured the Island, the Seabees went in and cut a road up this cliff so people could get in with materiel. Then they came in with all kind of stuff. We didn't know it at the time, but the plan was to make Emirau a jumping off place to take Truk. But since they came up through the Gilbert and Marshall Islands on one side and into the Admiralties on the other side, I guess things went a little better than they had planned.

Anyway, we went ashore there. We didn't really have anything to do because the carriers hadn't come in yet and they hadn't even built the shops. The Marines kicked out a coral strip and they started flying SBDs—that stands for Scout Bomber Douglas, built by Douglas Aircraft during the war. Anyway, the marines were hitting Kavieng, trying to keep the Japanese off of us. It must have worked because they didn't bother us over there any.

Then the Seabees started building a big bomber strip alongside the coral strip the Marines had put together. They put Marston matting and everything on it. Now that sounds like it should take a long time. But, shoot, it didn't take them Seabees but a few days on a coral island like that. All they did was knock down all the coconut trees and jungle off it, and scrape down to the coral, throw Marston matting on it, and man they had a good air strip there that would hold up heavy planes.

They brought in VPB 148 or 149. I'm not sure which. Since it's been so long ago, I've forgotten. VPB means it was a patrol bomber squadron. They started patrolling up towards Truk. But they weren't going all the way to Truk. They patrolled as far as they could get by with it. Of course, the whole intent was to find out what the Japs were doing. If we caught a ship isolated, wey'd try to destroy it. I think they sank two or three submarines and a few Japanese ships they'd catch out there. They flew PB-type aircraft that looked something like the English Hudson bomber, twin engine job. Pretty fast, too. They would really get up and go. We were there helping them out any way we could.

One morning the planes were getting ready to go out. We'd just finished checking them out, getting the IFF set on the right code of the day. This happened in early spring. A pilot stuck his head out of the cockpit and said, "Hey, Chief, how 'bout going with me? I'm short a man today." I had just made chief in February before this.

I said, "Are you serious, or just kidding me?"

He said, "I'm serious. We need a man. We're one short. Can you handle a 30 caliber?"

I said "Sure. Let me get a parachute."

He said, "The parachute's already aboard the plane. Come on."

I climbed in, and here we went. We cleared the island and they passed the word for everybody to check their guns to make sure they were working. So, I fired a round. We flew for a good long while and the pilot passed the word to keep a sharp lookout because the enemy had been hitting them in the area where we were. The weather had clouded up a bit. If you've been in the South Pacific, you know they have days like that, with low clouds and drizzling rain, although we had climbed up above the clouds. We flew on for 15-20 minutes, which means we had gone a good distance into the Japanese area where we could expect some action.

Where I was down in the belly of the plane, I couldn't see anything unless they came underneath. That was the object of this 30 caliber in the belly. It would only fire straight down or at a little angle outside. They had no other protection down there and tried to keep planes away from the belly if they could. I heard them say, "Bandits, dead ahead." They made one run on them. These fighters came out. I don't know if the Japanese were vectoring these fighters in or what, but they popped up right out of the clouds coming right towards us. They made one run by us and then this pilot of ours, he headed for the clouds because he was no match for three Japanese fighters.

When the guy opened up in the top turret, I had to abandon my spot for a minute or two because he was pouring hot brass down on me. I don't know if the Japs tried to find us in the clouds or not, but we headed home. It was kind of late when we got back. The pilot wrote me out a slip and told me I was going to turn it in to my outfit.

The next morning at Quarters, our officer in charge made the announcement that it had been rumored that some of us had been flying missions with the patrol squadron. He said that was taboo. It was considered being absent from your duty station without permission, which in wartime was a court martial offense. He said if it had been going on, he wanted it stopped.

Well, I had just made chief and I decided the best thing I could do was keep my mouth shut about going on patrol. All it would have taken would have been for me to get on report and I would have lost my hat. I would have been back wearing a white hat again. And I sure didn't want that. I found out later that old Lucas, who was our chief electrician had also made a flight with the Marines, the same day I did. He had been a chief a long time. So he knew to keep his mouth shut about it, too.

War is bad business. There's nothing good to say about men trying to kill each other any way they can. Still, it had to be done. I hated war, but at the same time I loved the Navy. It's a fine organization, and don't you ever believe anybody that says it isn't so. I enjoyed the work I did, and it felt real good knowing I was doing a job that was essential to the war effort. I knew how to patch up radios. After all, I had been tinkering with them for years by then. The best part was getting to fly some. I wasn't too keen on getting shot at, but that didn't happen all that often. When you're not under fire, there's nothing in the world as peaceful as flying. Planes back then were noisy, but the radio operator always wore headphones. I guess by today's standards they were slow, too.

Chapter 20: South Pacific

We held some Islands around the Solomons and Admiralties, and the Japanese were on some of the other islands. The Marines didn't try to capture every island in the Pacific Ocean. If they had, we'd still be out there fighting. Somebody figured out which ones we needed for air strips or to knock out something the Japanese had built, and that's where they concentrated their efforts.

I spent most of my time around Papua New Guinea, in places you probably never heard of and might not even be able to find on a map unless it's a real big one. Pityilu, Emarau, Ponam, they are islands out in the south Pacific. I was at some places so small you can easily walk all the way around them in an hour. Some of them are nothing more than a coral reef, kind of like a big rock sticking up out of the ocean. By comparison, Ponam is pretty good size.

Anyway, we didn't hang around on Emirau too long. They had invaded in the Admiralties and they were setting up an island up there to provide repair and overhaul for carrier aircraft. Of course, we didn't know anything about that until we got there.

There was a small island named Ponam up at the far end of Manus, which was the big island. There was Los Negros, Manus, Pityilu, and then Ponam. They deck loaded us on to an old merchant ship and ran us overnight from Emirau to the Admiralties. It wasn't very far. We went into the harbor there at Manus, and lay there on the ship for about a half a day.

They came in with landing craft and took us up and put us ashore on the Island of Ponam, where the Seabees were building an air strip. A good deal of the area was swamp. So, the Seabees blasted and dredged coral from the ocean bed and used it for landfill. While they were doing that, we were building and setting up our shops. It was pretty well organized.

They had everything we needed there. Good thing, too, because when we left Espiritu Santo we left everything there, just walked out, so another unit could take over. That was the smart thing to do. You wouldn't want to tear down and pack all that stuff and haul it all over the Pacific. We set up the station and had our shops ready to go by the time they started bringing the carrier planes in. We were taking care of the aircraft for the Marianas campaign.

Pretty much everybody knew they were getting ready to invade in the Marianas Islands—Guam, Saipan, and Tinian.

They built the airfield on Ponam, and that's where I spent the majority of my time. I was assigned to a couple of different CASUs. CASU stands for Carrier Aircraft Service Units. Our job was to get the planes combat ready. I maintained the radio and radar gear on anything that could fly off the deck of an aircraft carrier. That meant that the ammo and everything was all done, everything except being loaded up into the guns. And if they wanted it, we'd do that too. We had our own test pilots. One in particular I used to fly with when I could because he and I were pretty good friends. Incidentally, he was later killed in a crash. The plane broke in two in a dive and killed him.

We'd take these planes out and check them out. They would have an ordnance man in the turret, the planes that had one. Of course, the Curtiss SB2C Helldivers didn't have a turret. They were dive bombers so just carried a pilot and a radio/gunner. But the TBFs, which were torpedo bombers, had turrets. We would take the planes out, check them out, and turn them back in so they could be declared combat ready. The carriers with losses would run down there and pick up whatever they needed. They'd bring the carriers nearby and just fly the planes from the island onto the carrier. We stayed there for several months.

Ponam had been a big plantation before the war. The plantation owners and operators around that area pulled out before the Japanese took over. Either that, or they got killed or captured. A few of them hid out and became coast watchers for the US Navy.

Now those coast watchers were a bunch of brave men. They had to stay on the move because the Japs would intercept their radio signals and follow them to the transmitter. The coast watchers would send information on the position of enemy ships. Then they would have to pack up their equipment and lug it all to some new hiding place, sometimes another nearby island.

Some of the natives would cooperate with the coast watchers. Everybody was taking a risk, though. Generally, the Japanese didn't mess with the islanders. I guess they didn't consider them to be a threat. So, they let them be. But if they caught them sheltering a coast watcher, they'd butcher the whole village right on the spot.

The coast watchers had to be cautious, too. If one man knew a coast watcher's location and decided to talk to the Japanese, it was all over. I think those who survived as coast watchers were loners. They found their own isolated hiding places and didn't have contact with any other human beings if they could help it. They had to be real careful. Those guys had guts.

When we invaded Manus, they hadn't bothered to round up all the Japs. They just run them back into the jungle and cut them off from everything. So, they were over there at Manus, four or five miles away from us. They were no danger to us because they were stranded there in the jungle. I wonder if some of them didn't get back in there and starve to death.

Anyway, we had a chief bosun's mate who would take a landing craft and run up the river. He would take two or three sailors with him. They'd run up the river and switch off the boat's engine and let it drift back down the river. Every now and then, they'd catch one of these guys down at the river and they'd shoot him with their M1 rifles.

I know once they killed a Japanese soldier and he fell in the water. They came by and picked up his body with a boat hook. Then they came back and dumped the body up on the dock. Some of the officers went down there and threw the dead man's arms around their shoulders and had their picture made with him. I guess they sent those pictures home and told everybody what big wartime heroes they were. As soon as the officers got all the pictures they wanted, the sailors went down there. They were kicking the dead man's teeth out. So, the Old Man heard about it. He went out there and made the men take the body out to sea and bury him properly.

It wasn't too long after I got to the Pacific that Lucille wrote to me and said our daughter wanted to get married. Louise was mature for her age, but we still thought she was way too young to be thinking about marriage. What made it worse was the boy she wanted to marry was pretty near as young as she was. We wrote back and forth and agreed we would tell Louise she had to wait a year. Lucille figured it was just puppy love and would all be over with inside a year's time. I thought we were pretty clever by saying "wait" instead of "no."

In 1943 Louise came back and said her year was up and she and M.H. still wanted to get married. She was still too young I thought. But Lucille and I were kind of stuck. We couldn't go back on our word. So, Lucille signed the papers and those two got married. What a deal. Kids during wartime were getting married too young and without the long engagements my generation was used to.

Seemed like no time at all, Lucille wrote that M.H. got drafted and Louise was going to have a baby. Thanks to the Emperor of Japan, I was sitting on an island out in the Pacific when my first grandchild was born. If you don't think the men in my outfit teased me when they found out I was a grandpa, think again. They carried me high over that. I didn't care.

I was tickled pink when the kids named the baby Carlene, after me. They said she was a little cotton top, just like Louise and Leon were. As I said about Bango, she was pretty easy going most of the time, but all you had do is think about looking cross-eyed at that grandbaby and those black eyes would start to snap. Lucille loved that kid more than life itself. With M.H. in the Army and Louise with a baby to take care of and still just a baby herself, I was certain that teen-age marriage was headed for trouble. I expected as soon as things got a little rough, M.H. and Louise would call it quits.

How many couples can say they went to their daughter's fiftieth wedding celebration? We did, and I've got the pictures to prove it. I guess now Louise and M.H. are just waiting to collect a bunch of gifts for their sixtieth wedding anniversary before they split the sheet.

Chapter 21: Ponam

Sailors in my outfit used to gripe that the Navy searched the whole Pacific for an island where there were no coconuts. When they found it, they called it Ponam and stationed us there. Actually, it wasn't a bad place. You always have a small percentage of men who are miserable no matter where they are. If there hadn't been a war going on, I think I could have brought my family over and lived happily ever after on Ponam. I always loved those South Sea Islands. The heat never bothered me.

We weren't supposed to have anything to do with the natives on Ponam. The Navy put up a fence that cut the whole island into two parts. It went all the way across the island, right down to the shore. I never did see the point. I don't guess anybody else did either, because nobody on either side paid much attention to the fence. We just went out in the water and got around it. The people who lived there all swam and they all had boats. The fence was only a small inconvenience.

It was amazing how strong those men were. They didn't have big, bulging arms like Charles Atlas. Their arms and legs were smooth. But, man, they could lift anything. They could get out on the ocean in a little canoe-like boat and row all day. I heard somebody say the natives didn't have rippling arms because they built their muscle mostly by swimming. I don't know if that's true or not. I just know you'd be surprised how much weight some of those slender fellows could lift.

One of the Ponam natives, a young man, had been to Australia. He claimed he knew how to drive a car, something no one else in his village could do. Some of the villagers believed him and were impressed. The others said he was just making up that story. Well, I won't tell you how it was done, but there was an occasion when there was a GI jeep taken to that village. This fellow kept asking to drive. So finally, somebody gave him the keys.

Well, he could drive. He just couldn't remember how to stop. He drove around and around in a big circle, yelling for us to tell him how to stop the jeep. He wasn't going very fast. Finally, one of the sailors jumped in and hit the brake. We'd all have been in trouble if he'd wrecked that jeep. They were hard to come by out there in the islands. If I remember right, the only reason we had that one was because one of the men had stolen it for us. We didn't call it stealing, of course. It was known as placing a midnight requisition/

The Navy would have taken a dim view of all this foolishness, but everybody had a good time and nobody got hurt. People are all pretty much the same when you get past the differences in how we look and talk and dress.

Speaking of dress, folks living out around Papua New Guinea wore clothes that went from their waist to about mid-thigh, but nothing on top. That's men and women. There's nothing lewd about it. That's just the way they do things there. I remember one young sailor encountered a woman and got all embarrassed because she was bare-breasted. He took off the scarf that goes around that sailor collar and gave it to the woman. He tried to tell her it was for her to cover herself, but neither one of them spoke enough of the other's language to communicate. After some signs and signals, she finally understood the scarf was a gift. Well, this girl looked that scarf up and down, turned it over a couple of times, smiled real pretty, and tied it around her head. We never did let that sailor live that down.

Sailors stationed at Ponam got R&R in Australia. That's rest and recuperation. Men get pretty tired working hard every day without a break. After a year, we got to go on R&R and we needed it. Some of what happened I don't remember. The rest I've never told and don't believe I ever will. That was probably the only time in my life I went absolutely hog wild. I made only one entry in my log book for that time in Australia, "Drunk and disorderly, ten days." That's how long I was there. The yeoman kind of grinned and verified my log book entry without asking any questions.

Later on, we took care of some maintenance for the Philippines. Ships short of planes would come by there and pick up planes for the Philippine campaign. Our mission was about over there by that time, and they were breaking up the unit and transferring people out. I got transferred to a scouting squadron. Nothing was supposed to be revealed like this, but you could talk to people and piece together a lot of information if you worked at it. I started checking around and I found out that this Scouting 61 I was going to was located at Perth, Australia. Man, I was real happy. But it didn't do me any good. Fact is, they had left Australia. I met them over at Los Negros in the Admiralty Islands, just thirty or forty miles from where we were on Ponam. So I checked in over there and found they had no mission at Los Negros. They were getting ready for the invasion of Borneo, which never happened. We headed for Biac, but we were too early and they weren't ready for us.

So we landed over at another island—I forget the name—and were there a week before we went back to Biac. By then, I was the chief in charge of electricians, technicians, and radiomen, which were radio/gunners. We had eighteen SB2Cs and two J2Fs, which were seaplanes, amphibious jobs. single engine amphibious jobs which were used for air sea rescue. So, they told me, catch a boat and go over to another island and try to work out something.

That's how we did things during the war. Anything you didn't use up or need right away, you kept back to make trades with. Most of the time, I swapped for parts we needed to keep the planes flying. One time, though, I made deal to get a whole bunch of ice cream from a carrier pilot. I don't know how he laid hands on it, must have done a favor for the mess cook or something. You don't keep ice cream long in that climate, but that wasn't any problem. As soon as we got it unloaded, everybody just dug in and had a big bowl of cream. Nobody asked where it came from or how I got it. They just enjoyed it.

We had no shops, no maintenance, nothing. Of course, before we would be able to do anything, we had to be able to check our gear, check our IFF especially. I caught a boat to go the three or four miles I needed to go to see if I could work out a deal. These boats had no schedule or anything, and I couldn't get a boat back that night. Well, that very night, the Japs came in and bombed Biac. There was a lot of confusion later about how many planes there were. I heard somewhere between one and three. The soldiers had set up a movie down on the beach where it was all cleared out. They were just leaving the movie when the planes came in. They killed quite a few soldiers and did a good bit of damage. They bombed some warehouses and the tower on the airstrip. Then they were gone. The men on the island tried to shoot the planes down but they all got away. Incidentally, that was where Catherine Yeary's husband was killed. He died that night in the raid. I might very well have been with him if I hadn't been sent to do something else that day.

The other sailors in the outfit called me "Pappy" because I was so much older than they were. They were just a bunch of kids, really, not much older than Louise and Leon. I think they felt sorry for me because I was an old married man who had to leave his family behind. I never told any of them this, but I felt sorry for those guys. I had a chance to live a little before World War

II. They didn't. Some of them never got the chance either, because they never came home.

Chapter 22: Biac

I got back to Biac two or three days later. Our planes all came over there, although a couple went on down to Wadki Island. There were Japanese all over New Guinea, but they were all cut off and there wasn't much of anything they could do. Once in a while we'd do like they did to us at Biac, come in for a raid. Someone had reported that an enemy submarine had been surfacing out near Wadki at night and sending blinker signals over to the Japanese soldiers on the beach. It's easy to understand that they knew we were there, but they never came in while we were there.

The CASU didn't keep banker's hours. That's one way war is way different from civilian life. We worked until we couldn't think straight any more. Then we would grab some chow, sleep a while and hit it again. Even though we were behind the combat lines, everybody knew what we were doing was vital to the war effort. If we were ever in danger of losing sight of that fact, the Japanese would remind us. Those weren't BBs they were pumping into our men. Plus, now and then one of their planes would fly over and strafe our airfield or take a shot at any sailor they caught out in the open. Likewise, we knew some of the places where they were. When our aviators were returning from a mission with some extra ammunition, they felt free to take a little detour and give the enemy a taste of their own medicine.

Things weren't so formal in the Navy during the war. If a pilot's radioman was laid up, those guys never hesitated to ask if somebody wanted to take a ride. I tried never to miss a chance to fly a mission. Yes, it was dangerous. War is dangerous regardless of where you are. We all carried a personal log book where we kept a record of every flight we took. All verified, of course. You couldn't just write something in there without getting official authentication.

Those fly boys, they were restless. They wanted to get into the war one way or another. So, they decided they would make a run over a Japanese camp and strafe it. All they got out of that was a good chewing out. MacArthur wanted those places left alone if the Japs weren't giving us any trouble. I guess he wanted to let them alone to starve to death. Nothing serious came out of, but they dressed the pilots down pretty good. Among other things, the Island they hit belonged to the Dutch government. The Army wanted to keep the Japanese as quiet as much as possible because they still had some Dutch citizens in there and they were afraid we would provoke some retaliation.

We used to fly from Biac over to a little Dutch Island in this J2F we could land in the water. There were still some Dutch citizens farming over there. They hadn't ever been touched by the Japanese on their side of the island, although the Japs had a base on the other side. We used to go over there and get fresh milk and stuff for our mess. Sometime later, after they'd been down to Wadki, they got a report there was a ship in the harbor over there at that Japanese base. They got a notion to go over and try to get this ship. We went over there, but the ship was gone.

We saw what appeared to be a more or less abandoned air strip, like it had been started, never finished, and abandoned. But there were some airplanes down there. They decided to run across there and shoot up the planes. We made one run over the air strip. When we got down there, the planes were fakes. We still had some ack-ack, not too much. The guys in the rear were the only ones who could fire their weapons. The pilots hadn't noticed their ammunition was not loaded up. When you go on a mission like that, you're supposed to check your guns out, which the radioman usually would do. But the pilots didn't check their guns, and they found out their 20 millimeters wouldn't fire. So, they made that run over there for nothing. Luckily, nobody got hurt. This bombing, incidentally, took place on March 11, 1945.

After a while the Nazis surrendered in Europe. We were whipping the tar out of the Japanese navy by then, and I could see the Allies were going to win. I could also see we still had a long, hard fight ahead of us in the Pacific. I didn't know how long the war was going to go on, or whether or not I would survive it. Japanese soldiers were highly disciplined. You had the kill them or wound them so bad they couldn't continue to resist to make any headway. They never gave up.

I was still stationed in the South Pacific in 1945. I got to go back to the States late that summer, to a Marine installation in Virginia. I had been chosen to learn how to use some new radar equipment. Then I was supposed to go back and train a bunch of guys back in the Pacific. If you're up on your history, you know the United States dropped the first atomic bomb on Japan in August of 1945. You never heard such hollering and celebration as the one that broke out when those Marines heard that news. Nobody got any sleep in the barracks that night; I can tell you for sure. And I don't remember anybody minding much.

If you look at the pictures of the devastation that bomb caused you would wonder how in the world anybody could be happy about it. I don't believe those Marine boys were thinking about the people on the other end of all that atomic power. What they were yelling about was a reprieve on life. Those young men were being trained to go and fight in the Pacific. Based on what had happened so far, we would eventually win the war by making a lot of those marines give their lives to make that happen. The bomb short-circuited the whole process. All of the sudden, the end was in sight. Young men who thought they might not live to see their twenty-first birthday had a whole new lease on life.

I went back overseas and waited my turn to get mustered out of the service. I hadn't given much thought to what I would do when the war was over. I thought I would go back to San Angelo and get a job of some kind to support my family.

We weren't there on Biac too long before they started breaking us up because they decided our mission was complete. We ferried the planes up to the Philippines. On the way up we lost one plane. It went in the water off Peleliu. Fortunately, we picked up the pilot and the crewman, sent a gunboat out and picked them up. It took a while to get the planes to their destination, fool around with them for a while, and get transportation back.

When we got back to Biac, our outfit was gone. They'd all moved to the flag, which was down in the Admiralties. They sent all the pilots and crewmen from these 17 planes to get orders for further transfer. A few of the pilots came back to us, but most of them were scattered around. We ended up going to Pearl Harbor for further assignment. Twelve of the aircrewmen ended up getting back with us at Pearl. We caught a plane out of Los Negros in the Admiralty Islands. We weren't there very long, just long enough to get cleaned up and shaved and have a good meal while our orders were being cut. About eight or nine o'clock that night we flew out.

We ate breakfast at Betio, which was where Tarawa was. The Island's name was Betio, though. Tarawa was all secured by then, but we saw some of the Jap emplacements that made the place so hard to take. After eating breakfast, along some time in the night we flew to Pearl Harbor. The plane had to stay there several hours for a check because it was a pretty long flight from where we'd come. They had to check the engines and all. They went through our luggage and took away a bunch of pictures that I had. They took away just about everything anybody had that was of any value. I suspected people were keeping valuables for themselves. Maybe I shouldn't accuse them of that, but I think that's what was happening.

When we went back to get on the plane, there were some Army officers in our seats. I went up and asked the pilot what was going on. He said, "Well, what kind of priority do you have?"

I didn't know that. They'd given us a little old ticket from the Army Air Force. I showed him the ticket. He asked if all of had the same priority. I said, "Yes, Sir. All of the tickets are just alike."

He said, "Well, you people have ferry pilot priority. Those officers can't bump you off of here." So, he went back and threw them all off. Boy, that was a mad bunch of Army officers. So that way we didn't get held up.

We came into San Francisco, and it was all fogged in when we got there. We flew about 50 miles inland to some air base, and we unloaded. The white hats—I was the only chief in the group—the white hats were all wearing dungarees. All I had was some old khakis and a baseball cap with the chief's insignia on it. They wouldn't let us go anywhere around there dressed like that. We'd been out of the States for a long time. I called Alameda for transportation.

We had to wait a long time for the bus to drive out there. When it got there, we had a woman driver. She told us she had orders to take us to Treasure Island, so that's where we were going. We talked to her, kidded her all the way. The sailors had a ball talking to an American girl. I told her if she would just drive by the gate at Alameda we would get off and she could tell them anything she wanted to and we would back her up. She could tell them that we just got off there, because that's what we were going to do. She laughed and said, "Okay. It's no skin off my back.

So she took us to the main gate at Alameda and we never heard anything about it. I called from the main gate and got transportation to the offices at Alameda. Within twenty-four hours, we were out of there on rehabilitation leave. That's leave that didn't count against you. We were real happy to get that. We'd have been another month getting out of there if we'd had to go to Treasure Island.

We had to get uniforms and all. The next morning we got in uniform. They were cutting our orders, and I just walked out the door to get some transportation where I could get back home. Some guy yelled, "Hey, Yeary!" I looked over there and it was old Maylow, a guy I'd been in the outfit with at Ponam. He had been transferred to a cruiser when we left there. Old Maylow was still a white hat, meaning he hadn't made chief yet.

I waited around until Maylow got dismissed from quarters. Then we went inside and shot the bull for a couple of hours before I left. He had been up to Iwo Jima and Okinawa on that cruiser he was assigned to. He'd had it pretty rough. They took a kamikaze at Okinawa with a 1200-pound bomb on it. The bomb went through two or three decks and landed in a storage space but never did go off. That's the only thing that saved them. The whole ship would have gone if that thing had exploded. But they fished it out and threw it over the side of the ship. Of course, the fire from the plane did a lot of damage and killed some people. Old Maylow said his battle station was in the forty-millimeter guns on the fantail. He said they climbed up on the guns when the burning gasoline ran through the scuppers. He said he knew then it was time to get with it.

Chapter 23: Peace

I caught a ride out of Clovis, New Mexico, to a little store just north of where you turned off to go to the place where my brother Ralph and his wife lived outside of Morton, Texas. Some guy in a produce truck came by, and I got a ride with him on into Morton. Another brother of mine, Don, was living in Morton at that time, too. I went by and talked to Don for a while. He said, "Well, I'll take you out to Ralph's."

We started out and we met Ralph about half way. So, we stopped and he got out and we shook hands. Ralph had his sister-in-law with him. I looked over and saw that girl sitting in the car and I thought man, old Ralph really robbed the cradle. But it didn't turn out to be that way. We went on in to town and Ralph took Oneta's sister—you remember Ralph's wife, Oneta—on over wherever it was she was staying. Then we went on back to Ralph's place and visited. After a while, Ralph took me by to see Mama and then took me on home.

I got into San Angelo pretty late that night. I had 30 days leave coming to me. My daughter Louise lived with Lucille and Leon while our son-in-law was serving in the Army. I guess they kept each other company. I sure was excited to see that little girl Louise named after me.

Let me back up a little bit. When they were giving me my orders at Alameda, they asked me where I wanted to go. I said, "What do you mean where do I want to go? I want to go home."

The yeoman said, "No. What duty station do you want?" You see, I was still in the Navy and the war was still going on.

I said, "What can I get?"

He said, "You can get just about anything you ask for."

So, I said, "Well, give me Dallas Naval Air Station or Corpus Christi."

In a little bit he came back and said, "I'm sorry but I have to give you Patuxent River, Maryland." That was always the story. They never gave you what you wanted.

I never noticed when we left the Admiralties but when we went to the Philippines, they didn't send our log books with us. They were kept in the office and the log yeomen kept them. Of course, the books had already gone back to the flag, but I assumed they'd be with my orders and all. When we got back to Pearl Harbor and they were redistributing us, I asked about my log book because I didn't see it. They said, "No log book." It was too late to worry about it then. At the time, I didn't think it would make much difference. Anyway, I finally got home and took my 30 days leave.

At Patuxent River I got to checking and a lot of things had never been documented in my record. But without my log book I had no proof of any of it. I guess that's the way it goes. It was too late to do anything then. I expect somebody just threw my log book away. I'd been real good about making entries, too. Maybe someone didn't like the entry I'd made after a rest and recuperation leave in Australia.

So, I went to Patuxent River and I was assigned to service test up there, flying and testing airplanes. We were getting new planes and checking them out. I thought they were a little bit better than what we'd had before. We'd run all our standard tests and send the information to the fleet. We'd been down to Charleston, South Carolina, in a PBY, running from a storm. We spent the night on a little Marine Air Station along the coast of the Carolinas somewhere. The Marines in the barracks were partying so loud I didn't get much sleep that night, but I didn't know why until later.

When we got in to Patuxent River the next day, we found out the war was over. They told us they would figure up everybody's points and see when we would be released. You got points for type of duty you'd had, and your age and so forth. When they figured it up, I had so many points that I could get discharged immediately. So I said, "OK, write my orders," and I went home.

Of course, as soon as I got out of the service, I needed a job. I didn't have any luck getting back on at Goodfellow Field, where I worked just before the war. I wasn't excited about going back to manual labor at the transfer company, and of course Old Man Frank Van Court had found a new bookkeeper years ago. There were lots of men like me, coming home from the war and looking for work. Plus, a lot of women who started working during the war decided to keep on drawing a pay check. Seemed like there were ten men for every available job.

We weren't desperate like we were during the depression because Lucille had some savings built up and she still had her job. She had put aside all of what I sent her in allotments during the war and lived on what she made working at the laundry. Well, we always called it the laundry. After a while, they put her to work doing dry cleaning and running a big steam presser.

My primary skill was repairing and operating radio equipment. I could send and receive Morse code as good as anybody by then. There wasn't much demand for either one of those things in San Angelo, Texas, in the 1940s

I had stopped off and taken a test to get my second-class radio and telegraph license up in Dallas. After a couple of months I went on down to Corpus Christi, Texas, to the port there, to see if I could get a job as a radio operator on a commercial ship. By law, every ship of any size had to have a radio operator on board. I figured with all the commerce going on after the war, surely I would find some work. I decided I'd go to sea for a while until things settled down, because it looked like that was the best job available.

I looked in the paper the next morning and saw that Standard Oil of Indiana was advertising for a radio operator. They were sending a seismograph crew into the Gulf of Mexico. Since they had more than twelve men, they had to have a radio operator. They hired me and sent me temporarily to a land crew they had working close to Houston. They had bought a river steamer, an old stern wheeler, and they were using it for what they called a quarter boat. People would live on it. Their computer people had an office where the party chief and the assistant party chief stayed. They were compiling data from out in the Gulf.

I worked for Standard Oil for sixteen months. We would go out for ten days and come in for four. One day, I was in Houston waiting for them to get a new boat, an Army Air Force crash boat. It was about 65 feet long, a real nice craft. I was walking along the dock when I ran in to old Bill Andrews, a Navy buddy who'd been a quartermaster out in the Pacific. He was on recruiting duty in Houston. It was one of those chance meetings that can change your life.

He asked me what I was doing. When I told him I was working on a commercial ship he said, "Well if you're willing to go to sea, why don't you just get back in the Navy?"

I said, "Aw, they wouldn't take me back in the Navy. I'm too old. Besides, I was chief permanent appointment when they discharged me. Now that I've been out sixteen months, they wouldn't give me my chief permanent appointment back."

We made a bet on it, and then he took me over to see the Corpus Christi Navy recruiter. They weren't taking back everybody who had been discharged.

But since I was a radio repairman and that was a scarce skill, the Navy was willing to let me enlist at my old rank and pay just like I had never left. So Bill won the bet and I put the uniform back on.

Chapter 24: Chief Yeary

People don't believe I reenlisted in the Navy as a Chief, Permanent Appointment it, but that's what happened, after I stayed out almost a year and a half. I was always sorry about losing my log book, though. Lucille didn't complain when I told her I had re-upped. We were both used to doing whatever it took to keep body and soul together. I know she was lonesome when I had extended sea duty, but she would never have said so.

My assignment was to San Diego. So, Lucille and Leon and I packed up and moved to California. I was assigned to Air Group Five. They looked at my record and immediately reinstated me as an aircrewman. I went right back to flying, but my primary job was maintenance. I always liked flying. I wouldn't fly off them carriers now for all the tea in China, but I thought it was fun at the time. We went to Australia and all over the Pacific from there.

Back in San Diego, they got an All NAV (All Navy) message, wanting people to go to missile school. Included in the missile school was some training in television. I didn't figure they would even consider me, as old as I was, but I put in a request anyway. Believe it or not, I was in the first draft to go to missile school. So, I went to that eight or nine month school.

When I was pretty well along in the school, they picked out me and some other people and sent us over to the Norton Sound for a cruise up north in the Bering Sea. We went on that cruise before we came back and graduated. The Norton Sound was an experimental ship at the time, and later became the first missile ship the Navy ever had. Dr. Van Allen came aboard while I was there. You know, the man the Van Allen belt is named for. He had this idea there was a radiation belt around the earth, and he was running tests to prove it. He wanted to do some scientific experiments down near the pole having to do with atmospheric ozone. We had a missile that went a hundred and six miles high during those firings. That was a world record at the time.

Dr. Van Allen wasn't a celebrity back then, at least he didn't act like one. He knew his stuff, too. I went below one evening to check on some gear and there he was, electronic components spread out all over the floor, wiring up something he wanted to use the next day. I was so surprised I spoke without thinking. "Doc," I said, "I didn't know you ever got your hands dirty like this."

He smiled and said, "The best way to know how things work is to put them together yourself." He just kept on fiddling with whatever he was fixing. I did my check and went back topside. I thought Dr. Van Allen was a real nice guy. I always called him "Doctor" Van Allen, of course.

We went up off the Yukon River in the Bering Sea, and went all the way down the coast to the tip of South America, firing those missiles. We stopped off a few places and had liberty along the way and came back to the States by way of the Christmas Islands and Hawaii.

I got to do things and go places in the Navy that I would never have had a chance at as a civilian. Electrical things started being more electronic. Radar and nuclear power were new, interesting things.

Not everybody was like Dr. Van Allen. I remember some Navy expert coming to install a part on a piece of radar equipment on the Norton Sound. Right away I could see that he was putting it on backwards. It was supposed to cup inward, but this guy had it curving out. I told him I thought it went the other way, and he cursed at me. Well, sir, that equipment never did work right. People kept coming and looking at it. They would check a lot of circuits and walk away shaking their heads. Finally, some honcho from Naval Headquarters came aboard ship to have a look see. He walked up, kind of grinned, and turned that part around the other way. After that everything worked fine. The Navy could have avoided a lot of time and trouble if that first expert hadn't been too cocky to listen to an old enlisted man.

I stayed on the Norton Sound for about two years. One of my jobs was on the firing panel to fire the missiles. Captain Bagdanovich was the captain of the ship then. I was working on radar one day, on the way out for an operation, and he came by and said, "Chief, how long is it going to take to fix the radar?"

Well, you know, you have to tell them something. So, I said, "Oh, about an hour, I guess."

He went on. Much more than an hour went by, and we were getting close to the target area. He said, "Chief, I thought you said you could fix that in an hour."

I said, "Captain, I could if I could find out what's wrong with it."

That wasn't the answer he wanted. His face got red and his Adam's apple bobbed up and down and he turned the air blue. He was always on me about something, but I think he kind of liked me. He wouldn't pass me up without stopping and talking to me.

Some of the young sailors on the Norton Sound gave me a hard time about being an old man. They thought it was going to be easy when I led calisthenics, but they found out that wasn't the case. Sailors never got a pass on exercising just because it was this old man's turn to lead. I'd always kept myself in good physical shape, and I could do a lot more pushups than some of those soft young swabbies.

The Naval recruits kept getting younger and I kept getting older. By the 1960s there were more guys in the Navy who hadn't been in World War II as there were us war veterans. You could retire after 20 years in the Navy. Well, I was almost forty when I was called up. I made Chief Petty Officer after I was fifty years old. Some of those teenaged seamen thought I was older than dirt by then.

I remember one time some young whippersnapper started spouting off about Pacific Naval operations during World War II. When I corrected some of his facts, he said, "No, Chief. You're wrong. You need to go back and read up on your history."

"Read it, h—l,'" I told him. "'I *lived* it." Pardon my French. I was right, by the way. I was there and I know what happened.

Old Captain Bagdanovich made Admiral after I had left the Norton Sound. He came by one night at Point Mugu when I was standing watch in the hangar with the duty officer. He was a Rear Admiral by then. Of course, we were in a highly restricted area. The Captain came walking through there in civilian clothes. This lieutenant jg I was standing watch with jumped up and ran over there. He met Bagdanovich about 30 or 40 feet before he got to where we were.

The lieutenant said, "What in the h-—are you doing here?"

That was the wrong way to put the question. Admiral Bagdanovich let him know right away who he was and what he was doing. By then they were close to me, and I saluted him. He came on over and shook hands with me and told the jg, "This old chief and I used to serve on the same ship."

Afterward the jg started to get on me. He said, "Hey, why didn't you tell me who that was?"

I said, "You didn't give me any chance to tell you anything. You ran over there and challenged him before I could say anything." Old Baggy was a good guy. He was always raising sand with me over something, but that was his job.

A guy from Point Mugu came over to see me. His name was Ralph Hoany. He and I had gone to missile school together. He was in the guided missile training unit at Point Mugu. He said, "We're looking for people for the guided missile training unit. I came over to see if you'd be interested."

I said, "Yeah, why not." In about three weeks I got orders to report back to Point Mugu. I was there for about a week when they sent a group of us to Long Island, New York, to the factory where they were making the missiles. They were also assembling the APQ36 radar. They assigned Ralph Hoany and me to the APQ36 radar. We worked for the engineers there, setting everything up. They had a radar unit up on the roof. They would go up there and track a plane with the radar on the roof. It was the most advanced radar in existence at the time.

Anyway, we came back to GUMU41 after we got out of the guided missile training unit. We were assigned to work the VX4 in evaluation of the missiles, they had the Sparrow 1. Hoany and I were the only two who knew anything about the radar, so they immediately started us flying with the pilots, checking out the radar and trying to get other people checked out on it, too. Old Hoany went on and got a commission. He was a real nice guy. I was happy to see him become an officer. Mustangs, we call them. Naval officers who came up through the enlisted ranks.

I started out flying with a young lieutenant jg who'd just come back from Korea. I could tell he didn't want to fly with an old man. He'd get up there and barrel roll the plane, but I didn't pay any attention. I just went on with my business like the plane was flying straight and level. Commander Duncan, who'd been in Air Group 5 when I was there, he came by where I was at VX4 one day and said, "RHIP."

I said, "What?"

He said, "Rank has its privileges. I'm going to request you as a crewman." And he did. He told me later us old folks should fly together. So that's what happened. I flew with him.

We worked in teams, going out and firing missiles at a target. They had developed a real good radar system. The crewman would acquire the target and lock the radar on it. Then the pilot could just turn loose and let the radar fly the plane while he fired the missile. When he fired the missile, that released the mechanism that enabled the plane to take evasive action. If there was any debris from the target, the plane would automatically take evasive action. Of course, the pilots didn't trust it. As soon as they'd push the firing button, they'd push the release button, too, to take control back from the radar. They wanted to fly those planes hands on, and I couldn't blame them. Duncan was the same way. He didn't trust that radar too far, but it was real good.

I'd been around there a while and people kept talking about sending the missiles out to sea. I went and talked to Captain O'Leary, my commanding officer. He was a lieutenant commander at the time, but we called him captain because he was the skipper of the outfit. I told him, "Captain, some of us ought to go to sea with this to make sure it works out." I couldn't see sending a bunch of inexperienced people. You just knew it wouldn't be a success. He wouldn't say anything. He just kind of grinned. I should have known what he was planning then.

When it came time to send people to sea, O'Leary didn't go but I did. I guess he figured if I thought that way about it, I should be the one to go. They only sent about five or six of us experienced people out of GUMU41. I went to the Hancock. We got officers and men who'd just finished a sixteen-week school on the east coast. They didn't know diddly doo about nothing. The thing went sour on the Hancock and they transferred the missiles over to the Shangri-La. They sent a few of us from the Hancock to the Shangri-La. The only thing I can say is they figured some of us knew what we were doing and the rest didn't. They sent a chief warrant officer from Point Mugu to be the Division Officer. We had a lieutenant over at the Point who didn't know nothing. He wanted to go real bad, but they wouldn't let him go to the Shangri-La. Everything worked out real nice over there, under this chief warrant who knew what he was doing and let the experienced people take control. The guys that came from the school had just enough training to make them think they knew everything. I ended up staying with the ship.

Once Lucille got settled someplace, she didn't like having to pull up stakes and go somewhere else. So, as much as I could, I'd take sea duty instead of a land assignment that would have meant having to move the family. It was bad enough having to live more than a thousand miles from her nearest relatives, who were all back in Texas. I didn't want to make her move around like a nomad on top of that.

Chapter 25: Guam

Along toward the end of my tour on the Shangri-La, my nephew Glenn, Ralph's oldest boy, was reassigned as yeoman at North Island near San Diego. I got orders to go back to Point Mugu. I thought about trying to stay on the ship. Lucille and I had bought a house in San Diego, and neither one of us really wanted to leave. Glenn talked to his officer and he said I could stay if I wanted to.

Incidentally, Lucille had a good eye for real estate. I was wary about buying houses. A military family could be ordered to move on short notice, and I was afraid we would get stuck paying for a house we weren't able to sell. But Bango hated paying rent. She always said that was throwing good money after bad. She had shopped around in San Diego and found us a nice place to buy, solid redwood. It was in what they now call 'Old Town', down between the Spanish Graveyard and the Marriage Place of Ramona. She said she could turn a profit if we sold that house. So, that's what we did when I decided to accept my orders and go back to Point Mugu. If I stayed on the ship and gone to the East Coast, I might not have been able to get back to San Diego anyway.

We made a good deal of money on that house when we left San Diego, but I wish we had held onto it. It's probably worth a fortune now in that choice location.

My first tour at Mugu, we'd lived in one end of a converted Quonset hut. You know, there was a housing shortage right after World War II, with all those young men coming home from overseas, wanting to get married and start families. So, all kind of structures, including a lot of Quonset huts, got converted to military and even civilian housing about then. In the middle of the hut, the ceiling was real high, and then it curved on down to almost nothing on the sides. I remember Lucille had our bed shoved up against one of those low walls. On one side of the bed there was enough headroom, but if you took the inside, near the wall, you had to roll over to the outside edge of the bed to get in and out. Otherwise, if you sat straight up on the inside, you were liable to bump your head on the roof. Sound kind of reverberated in those huts, too. If somebody raised their voice in their end of the hut, you'd hear every word they said in our end. I guess there wasn't much insulation between the two units they put in there. Every now and then, you'll still see one of those old metal Quonset huts being used for storage out somewhere, and I guess people probably still live in some of them. They must have been built real sturdy. Anyway, Lucille went out and found us a dandy little house in Oxnard when I went back to the Point.

At Point Mugu, they assigned me to my same old outfit, back to GUMU 41. I took over shop maintenance again. They had some new missile test equipment. The missile program was changing then, where we got to just swapping out one black box for another one. I couldn't see that any technical ability was required. When we first started working in the program, we had authority to do whatever we wanted do. If we saw some benefit, why we could change things. Not without telling the engineers, of course. But we had a lot of freedom. After Sparrow One had gone to the fleet for evaluation everything was sort of locked in.

California sure was beautiful back then, in the 1940s and 50s. There weren't so many cars and people out there, although it seemed crowded to us country folks even then. There was some smog up around Point Mugu because it wasn't that far from Los Angeles. But nothing like what you have now. It hardly ever rained there then. Morning mist and ocean breezes kept everything green and lush. I've seen a lot of changes in my lifetime and one thing I can tell you is that we humans are pretty good at messing things up. If you don't believe that, just look at California.

After a while at GUMU 41 I asked to get out of the missile program. I wanted to have my rating changed to an aviation technician and go back to the fleet. After much cussing and discussing they finally agreed to let me put in my request. They approved it. I went to San Diego and was interviewed by the people down there, where my nephew Glenn had previously worked. I figured they would send me back to a carrier, because the tailhooks were mostly where I'd been. That's what they called the carrier sailors, tailhook sailors. But this fellow said, "Chief, we're going to have to send you to a heavy squadron."

I said, "Where is it?

He said, "Guam."

I said, "Well, I don't know anything about a heavy squadron." I was going to say 'but I'd be happy to go there'.

He said, "Sorry, Chief, that's where you're going."

I said, "Fine, suits me" I asked if I could take my wife out there.

He said, "Yeah, but you won't get concurrent travel. Your wife will have to stay in the States until you get a house out there." I was real glad Lucille could go with me to Guam. She took care of the kids and everything while I was in the war. After that, I'd done a lot of sea duty, and of course I flew all the time. I didn't want to have to leave her by herself again.

I went back to Mugu to wait for my orders. When they came, I was first sent to Barber's Point in Hawaii to go to school on the Cadillac system, which was the early warning system for the WV2s—the Willy Victor Twos we called them—and they were configured for fleet coverage. Had aps 20 search radar and aps 45 height finding. You could correlate the two and just play it on a radio screen or you could put it into a video transmitter and retransmit this information to the ships to play on their radar repeaters on the ship. It was pretty nice. So, I went to Barber's Point for six weeks to qualify for electronic crew chief before going on to Agana.

I got to Guam after I finished up at Barber's Point, and the division officer said, "Chief, what have you got in mind?"

I said, "Well, I'd like to be first radioman on one of these Willy Victors."

He laughed and said, "Well, you're not going to get that kind of job. You're going to be the new division chief."

I said, "But I just got here."

He said, "I don't care. That's how it's going to be. You're going to be the electronics division chief." And, sure enough, that's where I wound up. Since I was qualified as first radioman and also now qualified as an electronic crew chief, or ECC, that made me available to ride anything that came along. I didn't deploy quite as much that way.

We ran standby planes for emergencies. Like if we had a Russian submarine close by, they would break out the emergency crew and take the plane out and follow the sub. We couldn't do anything about it. They had as much right to be there as anybody else, but we flew coverage on them and kept watching them all the time they were in the Guam area. It wasn't a bad job. I know we had a Region Officer who was the commanding officer on one of the planes, and also assistant division officer. They flew most of the time and left me there by myself on Guam. I'd say sixty or seventy per cent of the time. And I took to assigning radiomen. I had to assign electricians and technicians and ECCs and all the rest.

As soon as I was assigned a set of quarters there at Agana, Lucille came on over, and I sure was glad to see her. Most of the wives of the men I worked with were younger, but she fell right in with them and made a lot of friends. I don't know why, but everybody said the bread we got in the commissary there was no good, no good at all. Lucille went to baking her own bread and pretty soon she had a whole bunch of gals she was teaching how to bake. She made the best yeast rolls you ever ate. They always came out perfect, and the whole house smelled good when they were baking.

During the time we were on Guam, they found a Japanese soldier from World War II living out in the jungle. It was in all the papers. He'd been out there for twenty years or more by that time, and they said he didn't even know the war was over. I never did see him except in pictures, but he looked real skinny. I don't know how he was able to survive. He must have been a real soldier, to go all that time and never surrender. I've often wondered whatever became of that guy.

I don't think Lucille liked Guam much, but she never complained. We had to keep a light on in the closets to keep our shoes from getting mold and mildew on them. That was because of the humidity. It's always humid on an island. If I could pick any place on earth to live, it would be on an island in the South Pacific. But not everybody feels that way, I guess.

We went to Japan for a couple of weeks. Lucille got a big kick out of the bullet train and bought some Noritake China. I think she sent a full set of dishes to Leon and Louise and a tea set to Carlene. She wasn't one to spend money on herself, but she loved to give to the kids and grandkids. When I'd get a break from flying and sailing around the world, I just wanted to rest and enjoy being home. Now I realize I should have taken Lucille more places. I wish I had.

One morning while I was on Guam I went down to turn in my muster report to the leading chief, an E-9. We were sitting there talking and he said, "Yeary, I'm mad at you."

And I said, "What did I do?"

He said, "It's not any one thing you did. It's what you do all the time."

I said, "What's that?"

He said, "Well, you've got a lot more to do with running this squadron than I do. I'm supposed to be the Leading Chief."

I said, "Aw, you're full of bull." I didn't convince him. And I guess he was right, because he didn't assign anybody. All he did was just sit in that office. It was a pretty good deal out there. Once in a while I'd have to jump and run. I know one time, we got a dispatch from the skipper, the commander of the squadron. He was deployed over there in the Philippines. The dispatch said he wanted Yeary and one other chief technician on the next available flight to Sangley Point. So, we went up there and we worked on the radar to get it working again. When my tour on Guam was up, I wound up going back to Point Mugu with the same kind of job.

Chapter 26: Texas Again

I loved the Navy. Oh, sure, I'd gripe about various things now and then, but I loved military life. Just flying, and fixing electronics and radar, and a lot of the time living in the tropics. I figured someday I'd have to retire, but that always seemed a long way off. The guys I worked with thought I was an old man, but I never had any trouble passing my flight physicals until after I got back from Guam.

I had a little bit of an uneasy feeling when the flight surgeon at Point Mugu put me through some tests I didn't remember having before. I asked the technicians what was going on, but I could see they weren't going to tell me anything. Then they called me in and told me I had to come off flying status because of my eyesight. I could see as good as anybody. At least, I thought I could. I never had any problem reading my instruments. They said it was my 'peripheral vision' that was the problem, and their diagnosis was glaucoma in both eyes.

I saw a specialist, and he painted a pretty grim picture. The doctor told me I was going to develop tunnel vision, and if I lived long enough I would be blind. They gave me some drops to put in my eyes every day. My mother was blind the last few years of her life from cataracts. So, I had some idea what I was going to have to deal with. When I told Lucille, she said, "Well, whatever happens, we'll just make the best of it."

I kept thinking the doctors had to be wrong. I thought maybe I had some damage to my eyes from radar or something else, and I didn't really have glaucoma at all. You know, in the early years, we didn't know anything about radiation shielding or protective gear or any of that. But every one of them who looked at me came up with same thing, glaucoma.

By that time, I had more than thirty years of military service and was almost sixty years old. I would have liked to keep on doing my job, but things were going to change whether I liked it or not. I would still be in the Navy now if I hadn't gone blind. I sure hated to retire.

I worked for a couple of years, and then we sold our house and moved back to Texas. Leon stayed in California, at least for the time being. He wasn't living at home by then, because he'd gotten married. I drove us back home in our

Volkswagen beetle. That's one of the most economical cars ever built. Ours was the old version, with an air-cooled engine in the back instead of the front of the car. I could still see well enough to pass those eye tests they give you to get your drivers' license.

Now, Lucille never wanted to live anywhere but her hometown of Lampasas. So, after living in Clyde, Texas, for a little while, that's where we went. I could still see pretty good, and I got a job working for the Army at Fort Hood. Lucille tried real hard to learn to drive, but it made her so nervous we both gave up on that idea. I had to admit that doctor's prediction of tunnel vision was starting to happen. I worked as long as I could, but after a couple of years I couldn't see to climb towers or do some of the other things my job required. Lucille walked everywhere she went, always had. I took up walking with her. I memorized the route and numbers of steps to places around town, like the post office and the bank. I got me one of them white canes like blind people use. It helped me find curbs and all, but the best thing it did was to warn folks to stay out of my way.

Lucille loved being back in town with her mother and her brothers and sisters. There was nothing that crowd liked better than playing cards or dominoes. I never could see much point to it myself. I'd rather have a good conversation than play some silly game. Lucille's mother lived a good, long life, way up into her nineties. The whole family grieved when she passed away. Old Belle lived in her own little house up there behind Lucille's sister's place until the day she died. Then she just went to sleep one night and didn't wake up the next morning. Her mind was sharp right up to the end. Maybe it was all that card-playing.

I set up my ham radio gear in the attic of our house in Lampasas. I spent many a good hour up there, talking to guys who'd been in the Navy, or fought in the Pacific or just shooting the bull in general. At the time, I could see to operate the equipment just fine. I was able to watch television as long as I was looking straight at it. Shoot, I could even drive around town with Lucille looking out for side traffic. But I could tell my field of vision was getting a little smaller as time went by.

Our son and his second wife had settled down out close to Abilene, and our daughter and son-in-law were living out in the country south of San Antonio. We'd had a good run in Lampasas, but in our eighties, I knew things had to change. The kids were after me to quit driving and turn in my license. I resisted for a while, but they were right of course. It made Lucille nervous to ride around with me, and I'd had some near misses that we never told the kids about. I didn't want to fool around and hurt somebody.

So, Lucille and I talked things over and decided to move out by Louise and her family. They had plenty of land where we would park a trailer, and our son-in-law, M. H., was real handy to fix anything we needed around the house. Lucille hated leaving Lampasas, but we didn't have any choice. So, that's what we did. We bought a two-bedroom trailer house and had it hauled down to San Antonio. M.H. poured a pad to set it on and then he locked it down real good with a bunch of steel cables. As soon as I could, I got my ham radio gear up and running.

We found a senior citizen's center in a little town not too far away. They sent a bus around to pick us up on certain days, and Lucille would go over there and play cards. Most of the time, I went with her. I could usually find some old man about like me to talk to while she was doing her thing. By then, I had also discovered that the State of Texas has a real good lending library for recorded books. I couldn't see enough to read any more, not even big print. The State sent me a player, and they'd let me have a certain number of books. When I sent a book back, I could get another one. Those books filled many a good hour for me. They had just about everything Zane Grey and Louis L'Amour ever wrote, and I think I eventually heard all of them.

Now and then, the Veteran's Administration would send someone out to check on me. One old boy—well, really, just a kid—came to see if I could qualify for a reading machine. It was one of those deals that you put something printed like a bill or a bank statement on top of, and it would read what the piece of paper said. He told me it didn't appear to him I could travel out to Phoenix, Arizona, to get training on the machine, which meant he couldn't approve letting me have it.

I asked him his age, and he told me. I told him I was teaching electronics before he was born. Then I said if he'd bring the machine out to my house and come back in thirty days, I'd have it up and running or he could take it back. No questions asked. He was kind of skeptical, but finally he agreed. Shoot, there was nothing to operating that reading machine. I was able to use it the day he brought it. The voice wasn't always easy to understand. You know, it was a monotone. And the way it pronounced some words was off, but all in all it was a real useful little machine.

We were smart to get situated there with Louise and M.H., because our health started to go downhill. Lucille had trouble keeping her blood pressure under control. I had always been healthy, but if you live long enough, something sneaks up on you. You've heard the saying, "Father time is undefeated"? It's true. I was diagnosed with prostate cancer, but they took care of that with surgery. I thought all of that was behind me, but then they found out I had stomach cancer. That time I had to do chemo, which is pretty rough business. I started thinking I couldn't keep on doing those chemo treatments because they made me too weak. For the last few sessions, M. H. came in and picked me up and carried me to the car. Then he carried me into the VA hospital for my treatment and back. I never would have made it if he hadn't seen after me. He was as good to Lucille and me as if we were his parents, and not just in-laws.

Well, I got through that cancer deal, and then Lucille started having some problems. For some reason, she didn't want the kids to know. I guess she was embarrassed about seeing things and forgetting things and sometimes making messes. After a while, they decided she had Parkinson's Disease. It was real hard when I had to let her go and live in a nursing home, but she'd got to where she didn't know right from wrong. If we didn't watch her she'd wander off from the house or start up cooking in the middle of the night when I was asleep, and then she'd forget about what she'd put on the stove. We put her where her sister Opal and sister-in-law Gladys lived. When my daughter or granddaughter took me to see her, sometimes she knew me but most often she didn't. But she always knew she was in Lampasas. We were married more than sixty years. There never was a better wife and mother than Lucille.

I knew a sailor who always had to find a pay phone and call his wife when the ship came into our home port. I asked him one time why he bothered with the phone when he didn't live more than a few miles away. He said, "I'm not going to throw away twenty years of marriage for the price of a phone call." I never had to worry about any hanky-panky with Lucille. She was a good woman. The best. I sort of scoffed at her straight-laced ways, but she just smiled and kept on going to church. Finally, she won me over and I became a Christian, too. When you've got a wife like Lucille praying for you, might as well just go ahead and do whatever she's asking the Lord for. You can't win against those two.

Chapter 27: W5YC Over and Out

I still have my original radio operator's license at Louise's house. My call letters were W5YC. The W5 part was assigned. I picked YC for Yeary, Carl. Of course, in voice transmissions YC is broadcast as 'Yankee Charlie'. You sure won't find any handles that short any more. If you do, you know you're talking to a real old timer. Of course, you can't do any ham stuff in an old folks' home. Now, I just talk on them cell phones. I've got a lot of numbers memorized. So, if you don't mind, I think I'll use your phone to Leon and Oneta while you're here, just to see how they're doing.

I try to remember to call this a nursing home instead of an old folks' home, since that's how they like to say it here. I decided I needed to move out of my house when I broke my hip. I told the doctor I fell and broke my hip. He said, "No, your hip broke, and that's why you fell." Anyway, that laid me up for a good while, getting over that hip thing. I still use a wheel chair a lot. My balance isn't what it used to be. M.H. had fixed me up a little apartment inside the big house he and Louise lived in, and he wired up an intercom so I could holler for help if I needed it. But they're not getting any younger, either. You know you're over the hill when you realize your kids are elderly. They never complained, but I know it wasn't easy for Louise and M.H. to have to take care of me. They couldn't leave the house for more than a couple of hours without getting one of the grandkids to come over and make sure I got fed. And then, after I got down so I couldn't even take a bath on my own, I decided it was time to get with the program.

The doctors thought I wouldn't survive that break, but they don't know as much as they think they do. That young doctor at Wilford Hall Medical Center tried to tell me I was too old for an angioplasty, too. He said the body of a ninety-five-year-old man couldn't stand the stress. I told him, "You put that balloon up inside of me and let's find out if I can take it or not. An old man wants to live just as much as a young man does." So, that's what they did, and I survived it. That was three or four years ago.

Anyway, after that stroke I had and then breaking my hip, I moved to that old folks' home out in Castroville. I picked it because it was close to Louise and M.H., but after a while decided to move into San Antonio so I'd be right here next to the medical center and all the doctors I have to see. It would take M.H. and Louise all day to come and load me up and get me into town for a medical appointment, and I have plenty of them. The Navy probably didn't know what they were bargaining for when they gave me lifetime medical care.

I like this location better, and I get a lot more visitors, too. People come through all the time wanting to cheer up us old timers. We had a bunch of high school ROTC kids in here the other day. They brought us a whole lot of candy and cookies that we're probably not supposed to have, but we sure didn't turn them down. John and I told them a lot of sea stories. Maybe they weren't interested, but they acted like they were and that was good enough for us.

You've met John before, my roommate here. He goes to his daughter's house a lot on the weekends. I got lucky when they assigned us to share a room. I don't meet too many guys older than me, but old John is almost a year my senior. He was in the Army during the war. We have a real good time swapping stories about those days. He likes to watch all kinds of sports on TV, especially golf. That suits me fine. I can't see the picture, but those sports announcers talk so much you always know what's going on. John's a big Tiger Woods fan. He's in pretty good shape, too. He pushes my wheel chair when we go to eat. You're never too old to make a new friend.

You might be surprised to find out how many of the workers here don't speak much English. I decided to check out a Spanish course from the state library for the blind and I've been learning a few words every afternoon. I tried some Spanish on one of the gals that gave me a bath the other day. She said I did pretty good for a beginner. I could have said the same thing about her bath-giving skills, but I didn't.

***

Common sense told us we would not always have Paw Paw, but our hearts did not want to let go. A military doctor beckoned me into the hallway to ask if I would "approve placing Mr. Yeary on a ventilator to prolong his life up to two weeks." Despite knowing I was carrying out my grandfather's emphatic, often-repeated choice, saying no to the ventilator was the hardest thing I've ever done. I returned to the hospital room to hold Paw Paw's hand while he took his last few labored breaths.

According to his wishes, Carl was buried at Dobyville Cemetery, next to Lucille, in his Navy dress uniform.

Carl William Yeary
1904 – 2003
Rest in Peace

***

I still miss my Paw Paw, especially on Saturday afternoons.

Billie's Poem

This is a poem Billie (Louise) wrote in memory of her father (Used by permission):
When night breezes stirred the summer heat
Through the trees like a simmering stew,
We would sit on the porch, the four of us
To rest when the day was through.
And Mamma would tell of the day's events,
She could spin a fine tale on a word
That someone had said, or something she saw,
Or bits of gossip she'd heard.
Then she would look at my brother and me
And ask in her softspoken way,
What did you do? Where did you go?
Did you learn something new today?
When all of that talk had idled away
And the breeze had died to a sigh,
Mamma would look at Daddy and say,
With a mischievous gleam in her eye
Well, Carl, what did you do today?
In the blue of Dad's eyes humor lurked.
As his mouth stretched into a smile, he'd say.
Well, today I worked.
With a poker face and not a trace
Of laughter that made it a jest,
I'd ask my dad to sing to us.
He'd shrug and say: I'll do my best.
Then he'd sing of bees in cigarette trees,
And a bum who was headed there soon,
In a flat melody completely off key
Dad couldn't carry a tune.
But we'd all cheer for we loved to hear
The nonsense that he would recite.

We didn't care that the tune wasn't there
Or that his voice fractured the night.
For we heard a far different melody
Sung by a father who cared
It wasn't the songs that gave us such joy
But the love and laughter we shared.
Dad would sing of buffalo girls who'd dare
To dance 'neath the light of the moon,
And yellow slippers he wanted to wear
That he'd bought sometime last June.
Then Mamma would say, if Dad had a box
And the lid was on it tight
He still couldn't croon, or carry a tune
And that was a terrible plight.
Dad would smile and sing again
This time of a silly clown.
The man was really king of all loons
And he came from Derby Town.
If memories could be bought and sold
For exactly what they're worth
There's not enough of silver or gold
In the whole of all the earth

    To buy from me one memory
        Of days that now are gone
        When my daddy sang in tones off key
        Some silly little song.

Other Books

BY BILLIE HOUSTON & CARLENE HAVEL

Discovering Emily
Old Maid Bride
Lucky in Love
That Scott Woman

BY CARLENE HAVEL

A Hero's Homecoming
Baxter Road Miracle
Evidence Not Seen
Parisian Surprise
A Sharecropper Christmas
Texas Runaway Bride
The Twice-Shy Heart

BY CARLENE HAVEL & SHARON FAUCHEUX

Daughter of the King
Song of the Shepherd Woman
Journey of the Shepherd Woman
Mothers of a Nation: Jacob's Wives
The Scarlet Cord

About the Author

Carlene Havel is Carl Yeary's granddaughter, and his namesake. She writes Christian fiction and sweet romance. You can connect with Carlene through her author page, https://www.facebook.com/AuthorCarleneHavel

www.ingramcontent.com/pod-product-compliance
Lightning Source LLC
Chambersburg PA
CBHW071310060426
42444CB00034B/1761